GOD CALLS US TO DO HARD THINGS

GOD CALLS US TO DO HARD THINGS

Lessons from the Alabama Wiregrass

KATIE BOYD BRITT

TWELVE

New York Boston

Twelve
Hachette Book Group
1290 Avenue of the Americas, New York, NY 10104
twelvebooks.com
twitter.com/twelvebooks

First Edition: November 2023

Twelve is an imprint of Grand Central Publishing. The Twelve name and logo are trademarks of Hachette Book Group, Inc.

Library of Congress Control Number: 2023943377

ISBNs: 978-1-5387-5628-7 (hardcover), 978-1-5387-5630-0 (ebook)

Printed in the United States of America

LSC-C

Printing 1, 2023

For Bennett and Ridgeway

and

the next generation

CONTENTS

INTRODUCTION

I'LL NEVER FORGET THAT DAY. It was a Wednesday. April 27, 2011. But for the grace of God, that would've been the date etched on my family's tombstone for the rest of time. Instead, that's the day our life began anew.

We were home, studying for the next day's final exams. First Avenue in Tuscaloosa. It was a quiet street of older homes occupied by graduate students, young families, and retirees.

My husband, Wesley, had returned to the University of Alabama to earn his MBA. I had also returned to our alma mater, pursuing my JD from the University of Alabama School of Law.

Those challenges were hard enough on their own. We, however, have never been ones to do things the easy way—or, necessarily, the conventional way. So, there we found ourselves both back in school with a newborn and a toddler.

Bennett, our daughter, had just celebrated her second birthday nine days ago that Wednesday. Ridgeway, our son, hit the 12-month mark 13 days before that.

Two of my three younger sisters, Janie and Jackson, were at the house with us that particular afternoon, as was one of my closest friends, Rob. Being from Coffee County in southeast Alabama, we were no strangers to severe weather. On March 1, 2007, Enterprise High School was hit by an EF4 tornado. Nine people, including eight students, tragically lost their lives. My youngest sister, Norma, was in class, but my dad checked her out of school and took her home before the tornado struck. My mom was substitute teaching at the school that day. She and my cousins were there when it happened. Thank God they survived as well.

Needless to say, we already took tornadoes seriously in the Boyd household on April 27, 2011. To add to our heightened awareness, Wesley's hometown of Cullman had been hit by a tornado that very morning. His two brothers, both fearless, big men, witnessed the destruction firsthand and reported what they had seen to Wesley. We were tuned into the threat of severe weather just hours after. When iconic Birmingham meteorologist James Spann said to get to our safe place now, I thought we were ready. Thinking of what we were taught in school about disaster preparedness, I suggested we shelter in place in a small hallway toward the back of our house.

We got there, but Wesley said that spot did not feel right to him.

He led us to a bedroom, to a small space tucked between two closets. James Spann's voice on the television called out our neighborhood. The threat was real—and it was headed right for us. It was at that point Wesley's days as an offensive lineman for the Crimson Tide and the New England Patriots really came in handy. We were surrounded by the two closets on opposite sides, with a wall to our backs and open space leading to the rest of the room in front of us. Wesley quickly blocked that opening with a large bureau, then he folded a mattress, held it over his head, and gathered the four adults, our two babies, and our beloved new puppy Dosh in tight beneath his six-foot, eight-inch frame. We could hear what sounded like a freight train approaching in the distance.

The power went out. James Spann's voice was gone. I cradled

Ridgeway in my arms while Jackson held Bennett. You could start to feel it.

Seconds felt like hours, and what must have been just a minute was a lifetime.

To this day, I still struggle to explain what it sounded like and what it felt like in that short eternity. Try to imagine being in a washing machine, with a rhythmic "chug, chug" roaring around you. The air was sucked from the room as by a vacuum. Our ears popped as we sang "Jesus Loves Me" to try and calm the kids. They didn't cry during all of this.

Finally, a flash of light emerged. We could feel air again.

I could see why when I looked up. The storm-scarred sky was the only thing above us now. The roof was gone.

Wesley moved the bureau, and we could see our home was gone, too.

The spot where I initially suggested we take shelter, what used to be a hallway, was decimated. The wind had violently funneled through it, blowing a door through its hinges and then sweeping up through the roof into the dark expanse above. There is no doubt that we all would have lost our lives if we had not moved.

Thankfully, we only sustained one physical injury from the tornado. At some point in the quick chaos, Wesley had put the mattress down. He said later that he was mentally preparing to catch any falling trees with his bare hands. Instead, he ended up just getting hit in the head by a Bible—one that was not ours. To this day, we do not know whom that Bible belonged to, but one thing was for sure: the good Lord was trying to tell him something. As Wesley will tell you with a chuckle now, the message was received loud and clear.

It was time for us to wake up.

Most of our house was totally destroyed. It was a complete loss. Our two vehicles were demolished. Most of our possessions were gone or unsalvageable. But none of that mattered.

We had everything we needed. We had our health, our lives. Our loved ones were safe. Our babies were unharmed. And we still had the opportunity to raise them.

We knew that we were blessed.

The tornado that tore through our home killed 64 people in Alabama, including a neighbor and a total of 44 people in the Tuscaloosa area. Our hearts broke for the families of those who were lost that day. That could've been us. By all logic, it should've been us.

We knew the answer to the question, "How are we still here?"

God.

It was the question, "Why are we still here?" that we had to answer.

Each and every day since then, we have woken up trying to answer that question through how we live our lives.

I'm here to tell you that every single day is a gift. How we use each day matters. How we use our opportunity at life matters.

Now, I also know that not many people on this planet get the stark type of wake-up call that I did—the type of singular moment that causes reflection on the very meaning of life. I want you to do me a favor as you're reading this. Take a step back and ask yourself the same questions I ask myself daily—"How am I using my life? What's my purpose?"

I did not arrive at the answer to that second question overnight. In fact, it's the journey to finding your answer that can be the most rewarding.

For me, I came to know that service is my answer. I never imagined what form that would take, and even now, I am unsure what form it may take in the future. I just know that I need to use the time God has given me to do more. With the opportunity to raise my two babies in mind, lifting up the next generation became my purpose.

The way each of us chooses to live our life impacts someone, whether it's ourselves or others. I want to use my time for not just my children, but for children across our great nation—and for their children to come. For girls like my daughter, for boys like my son: I want to preserve the foundational building blocks that have made our country so special and help grow opportunity for their future, so they can use their life to the fullest—and in the most meaningful, rewarding way. I want them not just to live, but to live out *their* American Dreams.

In this book, I hope to share some thoughts on navigating life and its many challenges by looking back at mine. What you'll find in these pages are the same lessons, ideals, and values Wesley and I are using to raise our children. The words you'll read and the stories I'll share form a memoir of sorts, experiences I've told thousands of students across Alabama about over the years—from commencement addresses, school assemblies, and class visits to Girls State and Boys State.

Now, I know that everyone's life story does not read like mine. Our journeys are all different. We each have unique backgrounds, experiences, and memories. Life can be messy—and that's ok. Certainly, as technology has evolved and times have changed, there are aspects of my formative years that young people today no longer experience at all or must grapple with in an alternative way.

However, what binds generations of Americans together—despite the inevitable churning waters of change—are the values and principles upon which our nation was founded. These are the beacons of light that radiate from that shining city on a hill, drawing the eyes of the world and guiding the hearts of humanity. They are the moral pillars of our society, and we must not allow them to be eroded by the harsh sands of time.

I am a walking testimony that life is fleeting and that we can never lose sight of what's most important. And in both the most gratifying and most challenging parts of life, ask the Lord and He will walk with you.

For the young person in your life, or for the young at heart who want to spark their own new lease on life, I hope this is a book that empowers, that motivates, and that helps you to do more.

Life is a gift. I'm happy to share it with you.

GOD CALLS US TO DO HARD THINGS

CHAPTER 1

A Leap of Faith

"FOR EVERYTHING, there is a season."

With those words in early February 2021, US Senator Richard Shelby announced he would not seek re-election in the 2022 election cycle. Instead, he would retire after six terms in the Senate, leaving an open Republican primary battle for the seat in Alabama.

Immediately, the question became, "Was it my season?"

The buzz among the political chattering class seemed to be that I would run for the seat, no doubt about it. That was their expectation and their assumption. The Associated Press article on Senator Shelby's decision to retire immediately named me as the first likely candidate to jump into the race. To everyone but my family and me, it was a foregone conclusion that I would be a candidate for the United States Senate.

Although that was the decision I eventually made and the rest is history, I can assure you it was far from inevitable. In fact, I had decided against running. Multiple times, really. The weeks and months following Senator Shelby's announcement were a decision-making roller coaster. I was in. Then out. Back in again. Totally undecided. Definitely out, right? There were days I could have flipped a coin, and there were days in which I was resolute—in competing directions, depending on when you caught me.

A lot was racing through my head and on my heart. My compass throughout this process was my faith, my family, and my friends. I prayed about it, and I prayed about it some more. There were countless conversations with family members, from Wesley to my parents and my sisters, as well as with my mentors and friends.

There was also a persistent tug from inside me, hoping that God would let me take the easy path—that God would allow me to stay in my comfort zone. Wesley and I each had jobs we never dreamed we would have growing up in Cullman and Coffee Counties, respectively. We were both from more rural parts of Alabama and never could have imagined enjoying the professional and financial success in which we found ourselves at 39 years old. At the time, I was president and CEO of the Business Council of Alabama, and Wesley was working for Alabama Power Company in applied innovation. We knew that to run for the Senate would necessitate us both resigning from our jobs. I prayed for Wesley's heart and mind to guide us, and—to be honest—a part of me quietly hoped he would shut this down and steer us away from jumping into the race. Instead, he was a rock throughout the process and my biggest, most consistent encourager.

What I knew I would be jumping into was anything but comfortable. An incumbent, veteran congressman from North Alabama was already in the race with a built-in war chest, expected millions in PAC support, decades of experience running for office, and the 45th President's endorsement. I had never run for elected office before and was, to the public, a complete unknown. Meanwhile, as the polls so coldly highlighted, he had nearly universal name identification, and the combination of these factors made most political wonks assume that he could not be beat.

To underscore that reality, I saw a poll at the time in which he was above 60%, while I was at 2%. Keep in mind that pollsters will tell you that any average Joe can stick their name on a ballot and automatically start with 4%. So, my 2% was truly extraordinary, just not in a way that inspired confidence.

This was a steep hill to climb. As I consulted with friends and political consultants, it became apparent that the general consensus was that the challenge was essentially impossible. At the same time, people warned me that opponents would attack me personally, along with my family. I was told it would ruin my career. I was told that if I ran, I would be a sacrificial lamb.

However, despite all of the conventional reasons why it could not be done and all of the risks and drawbacks associated with running, I felt the call to serve. I knew it was the right thing to do, and I knew what was at stake.

The hardest part of taking a leap of faith is that final step or two, right before you pass the point of no return and jump.

I think oftentimes when we pray for guidance, we are not prepared for what forms God's answers may take. Mine were delivered during this process through my children, Bennett and Ridgeway.

Their responses were especially fitting, because at the time—on top of everything else—I was grappling with particular tugs on my heartstrings as a momma. I knew running would mean being away from my kids more. It would mean missing some of the little moments of them growing up, like braiding Bennett's hair in the morning or running carpool from Ridgeway's football practice. I would have to miss some big ones, too, like watching them play their cross-town rival or not being home to hug them when they have a challenging day. I didn't want to miss any of it. I knew it would be a sacrifice as a parent, and I was praying for particular guidance on navigating this cost.

Ridgeway came to me during our family's spring break trip to DeSoto State Park in Fort Payne. We were in a small log cabin at the time, when he very seriously asked if he could "speak to me privately." Equal parts intrigued and anxious, admittedly feeling a little like I just got called into the principal's office, I obliged. He sat me down and proceeded to launch into a rather direct presentation on why he thought I needed to run for the US Senate.

This was definitely a proud parenting moment. He had a very thoughtfully laid out, exhaustive list that could fill several of these pages. They ranged from heart-warming, such as he wanted people to know what a good mom I was, to wise-beyond-his-years tactical reasons, like he thought my advocacy for small businesses during the pandemic would be the perfect launching pad for the campaign. He felt strongly that I needed to talk about work ethic, discuss where I came from, and tell my story. Can you believe this? My boy was 10 at the time.

I listened intently to the presentation. It was so thoughtful and well-prepared that I asked him if I could take out a pen and paper to take notes. After he wrapped up his pitch, I was candid with him. "I can't argue with any of your reasons why I should run. But, buddy, this is a really hard thing." I didn't go into every drawback or doubt with him, but they all raced through my head again. Mom and Dad would have to step down from our jobs. No one thinks we can win. Our family will be attacked in the press and online. We'll be alone.

"Politics is ugly. People can be really nasty. It's a bad business these days," I did tell him. Of course, he had the perfect answer—one that I now use to motivate more people to run for office themselves.

"That's because not enough good people are in it." We can't keep doing the same thing while expecting different results. If good people are not in the arena, why would we expect the outcome to be anything but bad?

That was one push, and one answer to my prayers.

The second came from Bennett a couple of weeks later.

We were at home, and she was a little more to the point than her younger brother.

"Momma, you have to run."

No presentation here, just the bottom line.

"Baby, I appreciate the confidence in your mom, but I don't think you understand—this is a really hard thing."

She did not hesitate, and with a twinge of southern, pre-teen sass in her response, I no longer felt like the adult in the conversation.

"Well, Momma, doesn't God call you to do *hard things*?"

Those words transported me back to spring 2011. It was days after the tornado ripped through our home and took most of our earthly possessions from us.

Our vehicles were totaled in the storm, of course, so I was driving a car borrowed from a family member at this point. I had Bennett in the back in a new car seat, which a friend was kind enough to give us after the old one met the same fate as our vehicles. We were cruising along, when Bennett asked me, "Where did Jesus go?"

My first reaction was of pure happiness. Here I am, with my

firstborn—having just turned two years old—asking about Jesus. There are a lot of days as a young parent when you don't feel like you're getting it right, but in that moment all the low points melted away from my mind. I must be doing alright at this parenting thing. My little girl was asking about Jesus!

Smiling as I said it, I told her that Jesus did not go anywhere—after all, He is always with us.

That answer did not cut it.

"Where did Jesus go, Mommy?"

"Nowhere, sweetie—He is in our hearts. He's always with us."

Now, I think you'll probably relate that when a toddler doesn't think you're on the same page, they will get you there very adamantly.

Bennett, locking onto my eyes through the rearview mirror, tried a third time.

"No, Mommy. Where. Did. He. Go?"

At this point, my proud parenting moment was in the distant past.

I pulled the car over onto the shoulder. "Bennett, did you see Jesus?"

"Yes ma'am. He played with me and RoRo (what she called Ridgeway) during the ronato (that's two-year-old for tornado). He was with us. But he just went bye-bye, and I want him to come back."

Now, here I was, thinking Wesley and I singing to the kids during the tornado had calmed them and kept them from crying. Nope. *He* was with us.

The faith of a child is an incredible thing. Fast forward to Bennett's words in spring 2021, almost exactly 10 years to the date later, and everything connected in my head.

Too often, we think of faith in the abstract. Instead, we need to remember that He literally will walk with us when we ask.

God does call us to do hard things, and He walks with us through it all. I knew what I had to do—and that we would not be alone.

While nothing about the task ahead became easier in that moment, everything became clearer.

We sure didn't know what the end result would be, but we knew it was time to get off the sidelines and enter the arena. *Game on.*

We came to terms with paying the costs of running. It helped by thinking of the costs of not running. This is something we can lose sight of in life, but the price of inaction—including the price of silence—can be astronomical, while the reward is nonexistent. Doing the hard thing is not only the most rewarding, but it's often the least costly in the long run. We have to remember that nothing good in life comes easy. And, from experience, I can assure you that you appreciate it more when you earn it.

We also can't lose sight of the fact that there is never a perfect time to take on a hard thing. If you're waiting for a flawless moment to undertake a challenge, it'll never come. Your arena may be very different than mine, but having the courage to step into it is no less important. We need a lot of good people doing a lot of hard things in every community across our great nation. Stages of life come and go, but there will always be an excuse of why you shouldn't do a hard thing.

It was a hard thing, but now I'm Alabama's first elected female US Senator, the youngest Republican woman ever in the US Senate, and the only Republican mom of school-aged kids in the Senate—a perspective that I believe is vitally important.

The bottom line in our calculation was this: if our generation does not step up and fight for the next generation, our children might not have anything left to fight for when they have children of their own.

Wesley and I looked around at the America in which we were raising Bennett and Ridgeway, and we didn't recognize the country that we know and love. The nation in which we grew up just three decades ago radiated optimism, strength, patriotism, pride, purpose, and possibility. While not much time has passed, a lot has changed—and much of it not for the better. I think parents in every corner of our nation are seeing the same thing, which is igniting an awakening of a political movement, from school boards to the US Senate.

It was morning in America when I was born in February 1982.

I am deeply proud of where I come from. Enterprise, Alabama. Coffee County. It's in what we call the Wiregrass—southeast Alabama right above the Florida panhandle and bordering Georgia.

I still to this day vividly remember what one of my dear friends since childhood, Stephen, told me my freshman year of college.

"Just promise me this: no matter where you go and what you are able to achieve, never ever forget where you came from."

I haven't. And I never will.

The Wiregrass, and particularly Coffee County, is a military community with deep roots in agriculture and fueled by Main Street small businesses. Faith, family, and freedom are the values ingrained in you from an early age. I am a fifth-generation Coffee countian and would not change that fact for the world.

My own family's experience runs the gamut of what makes it such a special place to grow up.

Growing up outside the gates of Fort Rucker (which was renamed Fort Novosel in 2023), home to US Army Aviation, we would hear helicopters flying overhead at all hours. That noise, to me, has been synonymous with the sound of freedom for as long as I can remember. However, I also witnessed firsthand the price of that protection. Going to school with children who had to move every few years or who had a parent serving overseas—some of whom never got the opportunity to return home—also deeply instilled in me that the sacrifice of our military service members extends to their entire families.

My paternal grandfather, PaPa, went to Marion Military Institute and at age 18 was drafted and served in World War II, deploying to France as an MP a few months before VE Day. He left the Army after WWII ended but would then rejoin for the Korean War, in which he served as a platoon leader and was involved in some truly brutal conflicts on the front lines of the fighting. Following the armistice in 1953, he transitioned into the Army Reserve. He would serve as the commander of Enterprise's local Army Reserve unit until he retired at age 60, having achieved the rank of captain.

It was his father, my paternal great-grandfather, who started a modest family hardware store right around the time the Great Depression struck. He soon sold boat motors and, later, boats. He opened up a funeral parlor, too—in his own home. Those small businesses stayed in our family for generations. When I was growing up, my dad ran the hardware store and the boat dealership, and he helped out at the family cemetery when needed. In all, he would work either six or seven days per week to provide for our family, grow his business, and ensure my sisters and I had the opportunity to thrive. My mom was an instructor at—and became the owner of—a local cinderblock dance studio and would pick up shifts substitute teaching when all four of us were old enough to be in school ourselves. Hard work and selflessness were my parents' nonstop MO.

I can still close my eyes and smell peanut harvest season. Nearby Dothan, the largest city in the Wiregrass, with a population of about 50,000 back then, is known as the "Peanut Capital of the World" and hosts the annual National Peanut Festival. However, it is Coffee County that is home to the area's oldest peanut processor, run by the Sessions Company. The home in which I grew up, where my parents still live to this day, is close to that peanut mill. The time of year when farmers would dig up the peanuts and let them dry for a couple of days in the fields before gathering them has a distinct smell that never fades from my memory. You can hear it, too. The mill would run peanut dryers during all hours of the day and night during harvest season. Peanut wagons would haul up and down every road in the county, from field to mill to market.

The peanut industry speaks to Coffee County's grit and resilience, too. Before 1915, cotton was the primary agriculture staple in the area. That all changed when boll weevils, a type of pest with a specific hunger for cotton, devastated the crop and the economic livelihood in the region. Yet, the people of Coffee County adapted, innovated, and overcame. They soon realized that the sandy, porous soil of the Wiregrass was very conducive to peanuts, and the rest was history. The City of Enterprise even erected a statue known as the Boll Weevil Monument in 1919 to celebrate the hidden opportunity with which the pest had presented the community.

Sometimes when life gives you pests, you make peanut butter.

I spoke at the centennial celebration of the Boll Weevil

Monument in Enterprise a few years ago. That may have been the biggest fanfare-filled event the city has ever hosted. But what more is there to celebrate than God's faithfulness? I am immensely proud that my hometown is filled with the type of people who live the words of Proverbs 3:5-6.

Trust in the Lord with all your heart, and lean not on your own understanding; In all your ways acknowledge Him, and He shall direct your paths.

My paternal great-grandmother, MiMi, helped found the small church we attended growing up—First Presbyterian Church of Enterprise. It sits right off the main road, proclaiming its enduring simplicity, heartfelt hospitality, timeless truth, and loving fellowship. I can still remember having homemade peanut brittle right after church every Sunday, brought by one of the congregants for others to enjoy. And even though it was good, no one's peanut brittle holds a candle to my Aunt Pam's.

The Wiregrass is a place where the concept of family runs deeper than biological family and where bonds aren't defined by genealogy. It was small enough that everybody knew everybody, at least a little bit. That also meant it was not just your own parents who would teach you right from wrong—someone else's mom was quick to correct you if you were out of line, and we were all the better for it. It is also the kind of place where friends become family.

I know that was true with my best friends growing up—Sally and Katie. These are the kinds of relationships that last life's seasons. Sally and Katie would end up being two of the three people to sign their names on the Federal Election Commission paperwork to formally launch my candidacy for the US Senate in 2021, almost 21 years to the date after we graduated high school.

When I remember growing up, what immediately comes to mind is my family pond house. This is where some of my earliest and fondest memories live.

It is on a plot of land that has been in the Boyd family going back to my great-great-grandparents. It started out as working timberland, then it was an active farm a couple of generations ago. The land surrounding it is still largely farmland.

At the pond house, the red clay sticks to your bare feet. It cakes the bottom of your boots and fills the creases in the leather. The smell of fish wafts up your nostrils, settling there whether you like it or not.

The pond house is where we would go every Sunday after church. It was where birthday celebrations were held, Easter eggs were hunted, and traditions were molded, like "Craft Day" the Friday after Thanksgiving every year. It was a place where generations of the Boyd family would gather. On Sundays, sometimes my parents would stay, and sometimes they would drop us off. My cousins would all be there. We were granted the freedom to be outside and be kids. The simplicity and joy associated with playing outside and entertaining ourselves for hours on end is a lost treasure. We did not hide behind electronic screens—we played hide and seek.

We snipe hunted when it started to get dark. Armed with only a stick and a paper bag, I would wander the woods for hours in search for those mysterious, fearsome "snipes." My older cousins took me on these hunts. They warned me of the dangers posed by those scary snipes. For a while, I couldn't quite figure out why the snipes were eluding me. As we moved through the trees, my cousins would point in a direction and say they just saw a snipe scurry by.

"There it is!"

"Where?!"

"Quick, look! Oh, you missed it. It went that way."

I looked high and low. I even tried to be quiet and not move, in the hopes that patience would win the day. But I still couldn't lay an eye on a single snipe. "I'm not very good at this," I thought in dismay.

Eventually, I discovered the trick to snipe hunting: *snipes don't exist*. Once I got the joke, it became my turn in the family cycle to help take my three sisters and younger cousins snipe hunting. It was a rite of passage and all in good fun.

We used our imagination and fostered creativity. We played on the tire swing for what seemed like forever. The world stood still, the only sign that time passed being the sun eventually fading from the sky. Getting dirt under our fingernails was the sign of a day well spent, and we'd come home smelling like we'd been outside all day, too.

But it was really the smells of fishing that take me back. We'd catch them from the pond, after digging up and hooking the worms and grasshoppers that we used for bait. We would scale the fish ourselves, so they could be fried on a pan for dinner. This is still a point of contention with my cousins, but I remember catching the biggest brim one day.

The house at the pond has its own distinct smell. It's an old-fashioned, small, dogtrot-style log cabin. The center has been closed in, where the breezeway once was, and some restoration has been done to maintain the original logs, which date back to the 19th century. Any time we were there, you would have family stacked on top of each other, but it was a happy, crowded feeling.

In many ways, I think the Wiregrass is representative of the American spirit and the American Dream—the dream that says if you work hard and seize opportunity, you can achieve more than your parents before you—and you can present your children with the same opportunity to surpass you one day.

The American Dream is not a superficial one. It is not about money or material wealth. It is about neither fame nor fortune. It is not even about outcomes—it is about possibilities. It comes down to the ability to achieve. And everyone's ideal achievements are different. The American Dream is anchored on the premise that there is endless opportunity for self-advancement in the United States if you live out a set of timeless, foundational American values.

For perhaps the first time in American history, that dream is at risk.

Even with all of life's valleys, through trials and tribulations, there is no doubt that I was incredibly blessed to have a loving family and caring community that ingrained in me the values that fueled my dream. Many American children today are not so fortunate.

Looking around, Wesley and I see the values that built our country slipping away. And we're not alone.

Parents are fearful that our children will have less opportunities and less freedom than we did growing up. Opportunity is being replaced in society by entitlement. Our culture now bristles at hard work. Instead of working with your hands and building yourself up, it is growingly popular to simply stick your hand out and demand to be given something you didn't earn. The country launched by the Declaration of Independence is facing a dependence-driven demise.

That's not even to mention the erosion of how we treat other people. What ever happened to the Golden Rule? We seem to have lost the innate ability to disagree agreeably as a society—a negative development fueled by the social media age. This is further inflaming a devaluation of our fellow human beings; it's easier to hate from afar, when you think of the object of your animosity as a username or a digital character rather than a person who has their own perspective, beliefs, and story. Ultimately, we're losing sight of the reality that there is much more that binds us together than what divides us.

It is time to stand up and say, "Enough is enough."

We live in the greatest nation the world has ever known, even on our worst day. And I believe that my story is proof positive that the flame of the American Dream still burns in our country's soul.

Against all odds, this public-school girl from Coffee County—a daughter of two small business owners—is a US Senator. If that isn't the American Dream at work, I don't know what is.

But winning an election is just one example of the hard things we are all called to do. If we are going to preserve the American Dream for the next generation, we are going to need a team of parents, budding young leaders, and hardworking Americans to get off the sidelines. Everyone's arena is different. Find yours. And step into the game.

Each generation before us has answered the call to defend the foundational freedoms and opportunity our country promises. It is our turn. It is going to be a hard thing. I won't sugarcoat it.

However, I am more hopeful than ever before that each of us will answer God's call, rise to this challenge, do our part, and get America back on track. Our children are our future, which is why our future is bright, despite the storms that cloud our view of the horizon. If we preserve our values, we will preserve the dream.

Remember, while this undertaking—and life itself—might seem like a lonely, uphill climb at times, God will walk with us. All we have to do is ask, with the faith of a child.

Katie, Wesley, Bennett, and Ridgeway standing on what used to be the second floor of their home in Tuscaloosa, Alabama, after it had been destroyed by the April 11, 2011, tornado. (*Stephanie Fisher*)

Katie, Wesley, Bennett, and Ridgeway in their home in Tuscaloosa following the 2011 tornado. (*Stephanie Fisher*)

Julian and Debra Boyd with Katie in 1983. (*Family of Katie Boyd Britt*)

Debra Boyd and Katie posing for a dance picture in 1983. (*Family of Katie Boyd Britt*)

Katie's grandfather Julian Herbert Boyd while stationed in Korea in March 1952. (*Family of Katie Boyd Britt*)

Katie's great-grandfather L. A. Boyd and business partner, Alto Hutchison, outside Boyd and Hutchison Hardware in Enterprise, Alabama, in 1939. (*Marion Post Wolcott*)

The Boyd family Pond House outside Enterprise in rural Coffee County. (*Family of Katie Boyd Britt*)

Katie flying a kite with her cousin on farmland near the Pond House in 1984. (*Family of Katie Boyd Britt*)

Katie and her cousins fishing on Boyd Pond on July 4, 1985.

Boyd Family Craft Day at the Pond House in 2021. (*Family of Katie Boyd Britt*)

Katie's maternal grandparents, Jane and Bill Donaldson, and family in Enterprise in December 2005. (*Family of Katie Boyd Britt*)

Katie's dance recital in 1996. (*Tommy Dunaway*)

Katie, Sally, and Katie in 1999, posing for their high school senior cheer pictures in Enterprise, Alabama. (*Tommy Dunaway*)

The Boyd sisters—Katie, Norma, Janie, and Jackson—playing around in Nashville, Tennessee, in 2007 at a show choir competition. (*Family of Katie Boyd Britt*)

BAMA BOUND

Katie Boyd
Parham - 305
347-4517 - Dorm
554-8390 - pager

THE UNIVERSITY OF ALABAMA

The note Katie gave Wesley when they met at the University of Alabama in the summer of 2000. (*Family of Katie Boyd Britt*)

Wesley's parents, Tommy and Vera Britt, and the Britt family in 2016 in Hanceville, Alabama. (*Leslie Dyer*)

Wesley Britt praying with his teammates ahead of a University of Alabama football game in 2004. (*University of Alabama*)

Wesley Britt being carried off the field and rallying the team and fans at Bryant-Denny Stadium after suffering a broken leg in the Alabama vs. Tennessee football game in 2003. (*University of Alabama*)

Wesley Britt, Tom Brady, Tommy Britt, and Julian Boyd ahead of Super Bowl XLII at University of Phoenix Stadium in Glendale, Arizona, in 2008. (*Family of Katie Boyd Britt*)

Senator Richard Shelby and Katie in 2007, when she was serving as press secretary. (*Family of Katie Boyd Britt*)

Katie and Wesley on their wedding day, March 8, 2008, in Enterprise, Alabama. (*Family of Katie Boyd Britt*)

Katie, Bennett, Wesley, and Ridgeway just a few hours after Ridgeway was born, on April 5, 2010, in Birmingham, Alabama. (*Family of Katie Boyd Britt*)

Katie and close friend Rob with Bennett and Ridgeway following University of Alabama Law School graduation in 2013. (*Family of Katie Boyd Britt*)

Bennett and Ridgeway with their great-grandmother MaMa at the Boyd family Pond House in 2015. (*Family of Katie Boyd Britt*)

Katie, Wesley, Bennett, and Ridgeway at the 2018 National Championship Game at Mercedes-Benz Stadium in Atlanta, Georgia, watching Alabama beat Georgia. (*Family of Katie Boyd Britt*)

Ridgeway helping his mom move into her office as chief of staff for Senator Richard Shelby in 2016. (*Family of Katie Boyd Britt*)

Katie and Bennett outside the U.S. Senate Chamber during her tenure as chief of staff in 2017. (*Family of Katie Boyd Britt)*

Katie with young supporters in Montgomery, Alabama, on election day. (*Family of Katie Boyd Britt*)

Katie, Wesley, Bennett, and Ridgeway praying together on election night, November 8, 2022, in Montgomery, Alabama. (*Family of Katie Boyd Britt*)

Katie and her family on election night in Montgomery, Alabama: Mamie Powell, Daniel Powell, Norma Boyd Powell, Chapman Powell, Chase Allen, Janie Boyd Allen, Curry Allen, Jules Allen, Katie Boyd Britt, Wesley Britt, Parks Allen, Bennett Britt, Ridgeway Britt, Debra Boyd, Julian Boyd, Jackson Boyd. (*Family of Katie Boyd Britt*)

Katie visits with students at Dunbar Creative and Performing Arts Magnet School on January 18, 2023, following her "Stand Back Up" speech. (*Dunbar Creative and Performing Arts Magnet School*)

CHAPTER 2

From Failure to Finding My Way

WHILE GOD CALLS US TO DO HARD THINGS, it's still scary. It's human nature to be risk averse. When we go outside of our comfort zone, we feel anxious or even downright petrified. We all know that feeling in the pit of our stomach.

The overwhelming fear of failure can paralyze people from taking action. We've all been there. The doubts creep in our head and can reach a deafening crescendo that overtakes our best reasoning and instinct.

"What if I lose? What if I'm not good enough? What will people think of me?"

We are living in a time of great fear. The pressures of the digital age, and the ramifications of people being constantly online and on guard, permeate our daily lives. Worry wreaks havoc on our decision-making, our conduct, our relationships, and our communities. We can be so afraid of failure that the desire to elude failure eclipses our motivation to succeed. Many times, this only holds us back from the very pursuits that yield true fulfillment and happiness.

But facing the fear of failure is an obstacle as old as time. And the answer remains the same as it was at the dawn of humankind.

Just look at Moses. Before he told the pharaoh to let God's people go, before he led the Israelites through the Red Sea, he was a man terrified to fail. When God directed him to Egypt, Moses was reluctant. He was sure that he would fail. He resisted and protested God's call, proclaiming why he felt inadequate and asking God to send someone else instead.

Imagine if you had no filter for failure. Well, it's possible. That filter is in your head—and only in your head—while the courage to tackle it is in your heart.

While failure is naturally uncomfortable, becoming comfortable with the potential of failure is a key to your future success. You need to embrace that you are not going to succeed every time and that failure is a necessary part of life. It is inevitable that you will try and fail. It is a cost we all must pay. It is unavoidable, so you should not try to hide from it. The trick is to be fearless of failure and learn by trial and error. And not all progress is seismic; sometimes it's slow and steady. It's incremental. But no matter what, it's forward. This is how you grow, overcome, and thrive in the long run. Think of failure as the toll you must pay on the road to attaining excellence—to achieving your dreams.

Failure is not the end of the process—it is an essential and healthy part of it. Ultimate failure only comes when you quit trying, yet success is achieved when you persevere through adversity.

I could write for days on end about times that I have fallen short. I once would've called those failures, but experience has shown me that they were really steps forward on the long, winding pathway to success.

These practice steps along the way range from public to private and span the journey of my life.

You might not guess it now, but my history of running for office is not exactly a spotless one. Sure, winning the election to the US Senate at age 40 was a big accomplishment. However, my initial forays into elections as a student ended very differently.

My first electoral failure was in seventh grade. That was the 1994-1995 academic year at Coppinville Junior High in Enterprise, which was originally built in 1960 shortly before integration as a high school for black students and called Coffee County Training School. Our band director at the time actually began teaching there in 1963 when it was segregated. He was at the school for the next 42 years. In 2017, that very same man, Mr. William Cooper, became Enterprise's first black mayor. In 2018, Coppinville moved to a new facility that sits right off of Boll Weevil Circle, while the old school is now used by the local Boys and Girls Club—an organization that I believe has the power to change lives across this nation. The modern building boasts storm shelters in each wing and allowed my hometown to become one of the first municipalities in Alabama to implement shelters at every city school.

I can vividly and fondly remember some of those days at Coppinville nearly 30 years ago. Each of the six city elementary schools fed into Coppinville. It was the first time I had a locker. The school was essentially a long L-shaped hallway of lockers, with classrooms branching off of it. Back then, one of the biggest worries in life was memorizing—and then not forgetting—your locker combination. Everything hinged on what happened at those lockers.

Coppinville was also when I first remember notes being passed around in class—and in-between classes in the hallways. We'd fold them up just so, to where you had to pull on a tab to open and read them. Notes kind of took on the function of modern-day text messages. They were more intentional than texts, because you had to take the time to write them and then deliver them. This allowed you the chance to reflect on your words before "hitting send." Plus, you were in the same room as the recipient and had to calculate the risk of the note being intercepted—or confiscated by a teacher. We'd have to be patient, waiting to quietly catch a classmate's eye to successfully advance a note to the next link in the chain. And, like text messages today, notes were a convenient way for people lacking courage to break up with their significant other. By the way—don't do that. It wasn't cool then, and some things don't change with time or medium.

We certainly did not have the state-of-the-art facility that houses Coppinville students now—the air-conditioned gymnasium, for one, would have been nice. But we had teachers, staff, and a community that gave us their best. They were dedicated to seeing us reach our full potential, and failure was a vital part of that process.

I ran for the student council that seventh-grade school year. I lost.

It was my dad who first spoke Winston Churchill's words to me: "Success is not final; failure is not fatal. It is the courage to continue that counts." He went on to explain to me that we must have the bravery to try, to fail, and to stand back up.

So, I did not let the failure, or the fear of a repeat result, keep me down for long. I attended Dauphin Junior High School in Enterprise for grades eight through nine. The school was in the same building as when my mom went to school there—and still is to this day.

Now, I hate to use the word hate. But those two years in eighth and ninth grade were rough times—and I hated it. The cute, gossipy notes of Coppinville's seventh grade gave way to mean-spirited threats at Dauphin. And lunchroom dynamics became all-consuming.

I remember walking into the lunchroom every day and worrying about who I would sit with. You'd enter the room and follow the cinderblock wall to the left, to the serving line against the back wall. The salad bar was on the opposite side, but I couldn't tell you what that looked like. I missed the simple days of elementary school, where I looked forward to square pizza every Friday or even lasagna now and then. I'd pick a milk or a juice, both still served back then in a carton. But in junior high, the menu was completely unmemorable. It was the early adolescent drama that was all-consuming. The lunchroom was much less about eating and more about social life. I don't think Dauphin was unique in this dynamic. In fact, ours was very likely similar to junior high lunchrooms all across this county.

I'd hope for kindness, as I anxiously searched for a welcoming place at a table. Who would let me sit with them today? Who would look away when I sought eye contact and permission?

I ran for student council again in ninth grade. And I lost again. The sting of losing yet another election and the fear of failure would keep me out of the game with regard to student government for the remainder of my junior high and high school years.

However, my belief in Churchill's wisdom was tested even more rigorously at 18 years old.

Being a University of Alabama cheerleader was what I was supposed to do. It was my destiny, or so I thought. I even remember as a girl giving my dad this plaque that had a picture of one of the University of Alabama cheerleaders and saying, "This is going to be me one day, Dad."

I did cheer starting in eighth grade and continued all throughout high school. I was *American Cheerleader*'s cheerleader of the month—and cheerleader of the year, landing me on the cover of the magazine. I was the National Cheerleading Association cheerleader of the year—and the World Cheerleading Association's cheerleader of the year, two years running. Who even knew that was a thing?

So, when it came time the April of my senior year of high school to try out to cheer at the University of Alabama ahead of my coming freshman fall semester, I was feeling good. I had done a little bit of special training in Birmingham to prepare for tryouts, and I even took on private lessons with a couple of the University cheerleaders. The travel around that was the first time my mom had been to Tuscaloosa.

Tryouts were in Coleman Coliseum, the 15,000-seat arena that is home to University of Alabama basketball and gymnastics. After applying to try out and being accepted, we made the journey to Tuscaloosa for the Monday through Thursday tryouts. My parents got a hotel room in town, and some family friends even made the trip to come watch me. It was a big deal to me, and people knew it.

At the end of each evening of tryouts, the names of those who advanced to the next day were read aloud for everyone(!) in the arena to hear. Those who were cut that day would find their names posted on a piece of paper. My name was called each night, until the last day.

I remember one side of the Coliseum looking about half full that Thursday. Final cuts were made. I didn't make it.

And I didn't make it in front of my family and friends. I failed to achieve a lifelong goal.

I will never forget that feeling. The plan I had for how I would spend my college days was not only gone, I knew there was no way for me to get it back. I was not only devastated because of what it meant for me, but I believed that I had let down my family, my friends, and my community. I wanted to be a source of pride for all of them. Instead, I felt like I'd failed them. And I was embarrassed.

After I made my way up from the floor into the bleachers, I thanked everyone for coming and then headed out the front doors. We went straight from Coleman Coliseum to the Arby's just steps away across the parking lot. I recall being so hungry, but that was not the emptiness that hurt the most. I tried my best to fight back tears.

This kicked off a formative time period in my life in which I truly prayed the words in Luke 22:42. "*Not my will, but Yours be done.*"

I was praying those words on stage the summer between my senior year of high school and my freshman year of college. At the time, I was Alabama's Junior Miss, and I was competing to be named America's Junior Miss (now the Distinguished Young Women program). It was a nationally televised event, broadcast live around the country from Mobile. The eight finalists were lined up in front of the crowd, and the master of ceremonies was reading the results, with the winner to be named last.

Second runner-up—another finalist, not me. Down to the final two. *Not my will, but Your will.*

Runner-up—my name is called. Not my—*oh. Ok. Really not my will, but Your will.*

I thought I had meant every word of that prayer until my name was read aloud at that moment. I lost. I was devastated. I felt like a failure. And once again I felt like I let down my family, my friends, and my community.

It was time to fight back tears again. I returned to my host family's home, where I had stayed for the two weeks of the competition. I felt torn. It was a real internal struggle. On one hand, I knew I should be grateful. I was trying my best to feel grateful—to truly be grateful. I knew it was not right to be fixated on what I didn't achieve instead of what I did achieve. First runner-up was an achievement. In my head, I knew that. So, why didn't it feel like it?

When my dad arrived, he gave me a hug—and that's when the tears bubbled up to the top. The tug of war in my heart hit its peak. Something objectively good had happened to me. But it wasn't what I wanted.

I couldn't see it at the time, but God had a different plan. He had a better plan. It just happened to be a plan that entailed my failing some more before finding where I was supposed to be.

FRESHMAN FAILURES

Coming into my freshman year at the University of Alabama, I was already scrambling for belonging and purpose. Not making the cheerleading squad left an immediate void in my self-identity and self-worth and upended the vision of what my college experience would entail. And I was tossed right into the deep end of finding my own way from the day I arrived on campus.

I decided to enroll in the final session of the summer semester to get acclimated before the frenzy of the fall. On move-in day, I was actually flying back into Alabama from a photo shoot for a cheerleading magazine. Ironic, I know. My parents met me at the airport in Montgomery. One of them had driven my dad's truck from Enterprise, while the other had driven my car, a black Firebird that I wish I still had today. It was packed to the brim with my stuff. My parents both had to work the next day, so they had to get back home. I was fighting back a flood of emotions, there were tears welling in my dad's eyes, and my mom told me to suck it up. If I couldn't do this by myself, she said, I had no business going off to school in the first place. They sent me on my way.

I joined a sorority, Chi Omega, after going through the rush process in August. I was a member of the Honors program and part of the inaugural class of Blount Scholars to live in Blount Hall—an experience designed to create a small, liberal arts college community tucked within the overarching university. Don't get me wrong—I loved the Blount program and living in that dorm. It fostered conversations that were collegial and warm, while also challenging and elevating. Still to this day, some of my fellow Blount residents are my dearest friends. Election Day at the polls was made even more special when I was greeted by one of my Blount friends and her newborn. These people and my experiences in the program helped me hone my critical thinking and examine my own beliefs and worldview.

However, socially, the dynamic of being in a sorority while being in Blount just seemed to exacerbate my difficulty of fitting in. Most freshman girls in sororities lived in an all-female dorm right off of sorority row, and my dorm was well across campus from there.

I would have to make the trek from Blount to the sorority house, while most of my pledge class were essentially living together right across the street from the house. I was disconnected, sitting on a fence post between two social worlds. Relatively speaking, I felt transient, or almost like an outsider—certainly not quite at home.

One of the first extracurricular programs in which I tried to find my place was Freshman Forum, a leadership development program.

I ran for president of Freshman Forum. I lost.

I was now—at least in my head—on a pretty major losing streak. Cheerleading tryouts. Junior Miss. Freshman Forum. I was 0-3.

I was hungry to find a place where I could belong, grow, and serve others. I got so desperate to find something on which to hang my hat that I tried out for Diamond Dolls, the official hostesses of the Crimson Tide baseball team. I knew absolutely nothing about baseball and had no business even trying out. It was pretty evident, and I didn't make the cut. I was 0-4.

On top of it all, I had gone into the school year thinking I wanted to be a medical doctor. That was my dream for years before college, and it was the course of study I had put myself on that fall. I thought medicine was how I could serve people. I thought that path was what I was supposed to do. However, the first day of my first semester, I knew that it wasn't the right path for me. But I didn't have the courage to change.

I brought my losing streak back to Enterprise that December for Christmas break. I was emotionally and mentally worn down, and being home made the hollow pain that I hadn't yet found my place in Tuscaloosa sting even more. Not only was I lost in the moment, but my long-term career plans—which I thought were well-laid and meant to be—seemed to have gone up in smoke. I wanted to make a difference and contribute to something greater than myself, but I could not find an outlet to make that happen.

I wondered who I was. I asked myself what I was doing, whether it was the right thing. Everyone wants to find their place, and the truth is that I was desperately trying to find mine. I even broached the possibility of transferring schools with my parents. I was ready to quit trying and almost bowed to failure—and the crippling fear of further failure.

It was my mom who really set me straight and helped me think correctly again.

"It hasn't worked out yet, but that just means this is preparing you for something greater," she told me. Not every single thing could be my thing, she reminded me. When one door closes, another opens.

I prayed for guidance, and I thought of what Jeremiah 29:11 tells us.

"For I know the plans I have for you," declares the Lord, "plans to prosper you and not to harm you, plans to give you hope and a future."

Not my will, but Your will.

I went back to Tuscaloosa in January for the second semester of my freshman year. I still wasn't quite clear on what I wanted to do with my life, but I also wasn't fully ready to abandon my pre-med track. I was worried people would think I was changing majors so quickly because I couldn't make the grade academically. They'd think I wasn't up to it. I reasoned with myself to give it more time. I did not want to be viewed as a quitter.

My next failure came pretty quickly. I tried out to be a member of Capstone Men and Women—the official student ambassadors for the University. This loss was delivered in nerve-wracking fashion.

My roommate and I both were in contention. If you didn't get accepted, you would get a phone call to let you know. If you did get accepted, you would receive an in-person knock on your door to congratulate you. We were sitting in our room one day near the beginning of the semester, waiting on this imminent news one way or the other. The phone rang—it was a landline back then, so we didn't know which one of us the call was for. The voice on the other end asked for my roommate. A couple of hours passed, and I heard from others who had received calls. My nerves began to be replaced with excitement—maybe I was getting a knock on the door.

The phone rang again that evening. My heart sank. It was for me. A lump swelled in my throat, as I tried mightily to respond with a clear head and a gracious heart. I was not accepted. My voice could not help but tremble as I sought to mask my devastation. I was second alternate. Oh-so close. 0-5.

I started to wonder if I would ever find my place and have the opportunity to contribute to something meaningful—something bigger than myself. I prayed some more. I searched some more. And I finally found my answer.

Student Government Association elections followed closely on the heels of the Capstone Men and Women disappointment. A student who was a couple of years older and also from Coffee County knew I was struggling, so she suggested that I consider running for a spot in the student senate. SGA is very active on campus, and it's a great way to develop leadership skills, she told me. I think you're right for it, she added.

But the last time I went down this road, I had failed.

And before that interaction, I had honestly never thought of SGA as something attainable for me. SGA at the University of Alabama had the reputation at the time of being exclusive to the children of storied families across the state—those from the most prestigious high schools, whose parents walked Alabama's halls of power and had the bank accounts to match. Then there was me.

My dad had attended the University of West Alabama (which was called Livingston University back in his day) and then Troy University. My mom did not have the opportunity to go off to college. My parents were hardworking small business owners. They were not political donors and were not connected to the powers-that-be at the University. They taught me to treat people right and to respect the dignity of an honest day's work. I was attending school with funds I earned from a multitude of competitive scholarship programs. We were not blue bloods by the standards set forth at the University. So, when I first heard how exclusive SGA was, I assumed it would be out of reach for this girl from the Wiregrass.

But the suggestion to run for the student senate flipped my perspective. It gave me confidence. My friend knew me. My friend knew about my failures but still believed in what was possible. That helped remind me what I was capable of, and no doubt her encouragement inspired me to prove it.

I worked harder than I had ever worked before on that SGA Senate campaign. I paid attention to every detail. This opportunity felt different. And I wasn't going to let it slip through my fingers because I was outworked. I chalked the sidewalks of the Quad, dug into the issues, learned what fellow students were concerned about, asked people for their votes nonstop, and was willing to show up in unlikely places.

At the end of the day, it paid off. I won. I was a Senator—for the College of Arts and Sciences.

I quickly realized that I had found my place. Rather, maybe, it found me. We are all looking for a place to belong, and for the first time in a long time I felt like I belonged. I had purpose and meaning on campus. I was passionate about what I was doing—that it mattered and that I could make a positive difference for others.

I loved the little things about SGA—the seemingly small, everyday aspects of student life that I could improve, make more efficient and more accessible. I made sure to spend time in the SGA office to listen and learn. I poured myself into the service mission of it all, and the greatest gratification was speaking with students whom I was able to help directly.

The next spring, I worked to build support from every corner of campus and ran for Vice President for Student Affairs of the SGA. This time I was unopposed.

While many people thought I already had my eyes set on being SGA President, the truth is that it wasn't until after a forum when I was running for Vice President for Student Affairs that I made my decision about what the next year would entail.

A good friend of mine came up to me after it was over to tell me what a nice job I had done. "You did a really great job up there," he said. I was a little taken back because he wasn't one to offer up compliments with any ease. I told him thank you and how much I appreciated him being there. Shaking his head in affirmation he continued, "No, seriously. You're really good at this." I told him once again that I appreciated it, and I almost started to settle into the compliment—and then he came with it.

"It's too bad you won't go any further."

I was a bit startled and immediately asked him what he was talking about—after all, he just told me how *good* I was at this. He went on to explain, "Well, you won't go any further, you know, because you're a girl." It was in that *very* moment that I decided I would run for SGA President, no matter what. People could beat me or join me. But I was determined to prove him wrong. There was no world in which I was going to be told "no" because I am a girl. *Game on.*

My junior year, I pushed forward and ran for SGA President. I worked my tail off, campaigning to student organizations in every corner of campus life. And I won. There were questions on the integrity of the balloting, so I called for a new election. And I won again.

That spring, I applied to intern in Washington, DC, for Senator Shelby through a political science department class credit. SGA had gotten me hooked on government, and I wanted to see if governmental service outside the confines of campus was for me.

I got the internship for that summer before my senior year of college, and the rest, I suppose, is history. Except that I thought my greatest contribution in government would be *working* for an elected official, not actually *being* the elected official. While there was always part of me that deep down wondered, the truth is that, once again, I assumed that would be out of reach.

Looking back, God's plan was at work the entire time. It was better than my plan all along. I just couldn't see it while in the moment.

VALLEYS MAKE PEAKS POSSIBLE

Let's examine how my failures were part of God's plan—and how I would not have succeeded if not for those failures.

It's not an exaggeration to say that I would not be a US Senator today if not for each and every one of those failures. If I would have gotten just one of those things I tried for, I would not have run for the student senate my freshman year. Which means I wouldn't have gotten so involved in SGA my collegiate career, which means I would not have interned for Senator Shelby, which means I never would have worked in his office, which means I never would have run to succeed him in the US Senate.

Cheerleader. Junior Miss. Freshman Forum. Diamond Dolls. Pre-med. Capstone Men and Women.

They were not the right things for me. And, in fact, they would have gotten in the way of what was the right thing—of what was God's plan. These failures pushed me in different directions—albeit ones that were frustrating in the moment.

We have to remind ourselves that sometimes God gets us out of our lane and lights up another one because he knows we are too fearful to do it ourselves.

And ultimately, God's plans for us are better than the best-laid plans we can make for ourselves. So, don't be fearful of God's will, even if it's different from yours—and even if it includes failure along the journey.

The world sees our peaks, but God knows our valleys. And, while those peaks are often fun, the valleys shape and define us. The valleys are where He carves us—and builds us up.

The key to growing in those valleys is to be honest about how you got there or what you could have done differently. Admitting weakness is actually a strength if you're committed to learning and taking action to improve. Take ownership and reflect on what you need to change to avoid a repeat result in the future. Then, make that change.

One of the failures I learned from the most was running for president of Freshman Forum. I was actually running against my roommate, Elizabeth, who to this day is a great friend. Before the election, I was approached by someone who told me I could attach myself to an existing campaign effort that was already organized and moving, essentially giving me a shortcut. I made the wrong decision and chose to rely on others rather than doing the work myself. I took the shortcut and I lost.

And I should have. In the end, I was disappointed in myself, because I knew better. Instead of working hard, I sat back and assumed I would succeed. That was a lesson I never forgot and my disappointment in myself still stings. You have to earn it. People don't—and shouldn't—respect you otherwise. Elizabeth worked the vote and deserved to win. She won the right way. She was a true leader and had the courage to do hard things.

Capstone Men and Women held a similar message for me. The process to become one of these University ambassadors centers on in-person interviews, in which you are faced with random, off-the-wall scenarios and questions you might have to face in giving a campus tour or interacting with a prospective student or a prospective student's family. I felt the pressure of the interview, and—in becoming too worried about reciting "the right answer"—I lost sight of being my authentic self. My takeaway afterward was to stick to my beliefs and be confident in sharing what I knew—whether the audience agrees or not.

These failures were painful in the moment. But they were necessary and useful, because I learned from them, grew, and didn't let the fear of failing again stop me from getting back on the horse. Having faced plenty of it myself, I can say without a doubt that you have to face defeat in order to truly appreciate victory.

In fact, many of the people our society considers the most successful have reached the pinnacle of achievement because the agony of previous defeats—of past failures—has motivated them to avoid repeat performances.

That's one of the weaknesses created by the participation trophy mentality our society has recently nurtured. When everyone is told they won, lessons are harder to learn. And when that is the case, no one *actually* wins.

I've seen a championship mindset up close when Wesley played for Bill Belichick's New England Patriots. And it's a far cry from this latest generation of helicopter parents determined to insulate young people from feelings of failure.

Embrace competition. Know that iron really does sharpen iron. Be unafraid to fail. And know that it's ok when you do—as long as you respond to it properly.

Remember: nobody is born perfect, and despite our best efforts, we will never reach being free of all failure. It is unrealistic and unhealthy to think otherwise. Being a lifelong learner includes constantly gaining knowledge from our own mistakes and growing as a result of our constructive self-evaluation.

When we see leading names throughout history, in popular culture, or even in our own professional sectors, we subconsciously idealize these figures, equating them with success—and even perfection. However, the candid life stories behind these names reveal the struggles, the adversity, and the failures these individuals faced down and overcame to become household names.

Michael Jordan failed to make the varsity basketball team his sophomore year in high school. Einstein failed his first collegiate entrance exam, and he nearly dropped out after he was admitted. Oprah was fired from her first TV job. Dr. Seuss had his first book rejected by 27 different publishers. Elvis was canned after his first performance at the Grand Ole Opry.

The examples could run on for pages. The simple truth is that the master has failed more times than the novice has even dreamed of trying.

No one enjoys failing. However, failure is an inevitability. The truth is that it is not *if*, but *when* we will fail or fall short next. Great leaders, and people who accomplish hard things, are molded by knowing that we are not defined by our failures or our missteps. They do not attempt to cover up or conceal their failures. Instead, they honestly analyze what went wrong and make a dogged effort to correct and improve. It is not how you fall, but how you stand back up.

That habit of great leaders goes even further. In fact, even in moments of short-term success, we should be seeking out ways to constantly grow, improve, and advance ourselves. If we know we could have done something better or in a better way, even if we got the desired result this time, we should be laser-focused on making a positive change. Because next time, the result could be failure—and it could have been avoidable if we had been in a mode of constant growth.

There is considerable value in learning from our mistakes and our shortcomings. This mindset—the one that is comfortable with the concept of failure and that knows how to use failure to improve—can lay the foundation to achieve our dreams.

President Reagan once said that "America's future rests in a thousand dreams inside your hearts."

Whether dreams come to fruition or lie dormant inside of us depends on the *courage to dare*. That is at the heart of the American spirit. Our country, built on the rallying cry, "Give me liberty or give me death," was born out of a founding mentality of having a courageous heart and being unafraid to fail.

This underlying national identity is not just what paved the way to our past and present. Facing failure head-on will determine whether America remains the greatest nation ever known to the world, or whether we become another history lesson akin to the Roman Empire.

Across the globe, we face growing challenges—including our greatest national security and geopolitical threat, the Chinese Communist Party. Here at home, we're confronted with a litany of domestic issues that are crushing hardworking American families. From an unprecedented fentanyl crisis and the historic mental health epidemic to an eroding culture of violence and a ballooning national debt, fear-induced paralysis produces only inaction. Especially in a time such as this, we need boldness. We need innovative solutions and people willing to do the hard things necessary to implement them. We need leaders who are not fearful of failure—who stare down setbacks, learn from them, and then find a way to prevail moving forward.

If I had let the fear of failure win the day, I would certainly not be a US Senator. Even as a 39-year-old woman deliberating whether or not to seek a Senate seat, the specter of not succeeding still haunted me. This is a constant struggle—one that I confront on a daily basis. It is something of which I am vigilant as I introduce legislation, as I take on executive branch overreach, and as I fight for Alabama's and America's people, interests, and values.

I'm a US Senator. And I can still fail. No, I *do* still fail.

It still isn't fun. That truth doesn't necessarily change with age or experience. But it does get easier when we learn to accept failure as the cost of growing, of succeeding, and of living our dreams.

Isaiah 41:13 tells us, "*For I am the Lord your God who takes hold of your right hand and says to you, 'Fear not; for I am with you.'*"

Failure is timeless. But time and time again, we do hard things by being unafraid and asking Him to walk with us.

Take a deep breath and pray these words with me: "Not my will, but Yours be done."

Now, take His hand and walk forward with comfort, knowing His plan is at work.

CHAPTER 3

Be You

GOD CALLS US TO BE OURSELVES—the best version of ourselves—and that's a hard thing.

Society places constant pressure on us, pushing and pulling in every direction imaginable. We're told what we should think, how we should act, and who we should be.

It's natural to look around and compare ourselves to others, whether you're still in school or keeping up with the Joneses next door. The easy thing is to try and be more like everyone else. Our instincts tell us that fitting in with the pack is comfortable. Conforming feels safe.

But one of the greatest privileges you will ever have is the freedom to be *yourself.*

Exercising this freedom is within our power every day. However, it is easier said than done.

Above all else, I always work to keep at the top of my mind *whose* I am—our Lord and Savior, Jesus Christ. You are made in God's image. Never lose sight of that.

From there, the next step is to keep in mind what you are called to do—not necessarily what is expected of you by others.

The words of Romans 12:2 are a powerful guide.

Do not be conformed to this world, but be transformed by the renewal of your mind, that by testing you may discern what is the will of God, what is good and acceptable and perfect.

It would have been easy for my parents to raise my three sisters and me to be the same—to do the same things and have the same hobbies. We are all relatively close in age. I am the oldest, then Jackson, then Janie, then Norma. My parents both worked constantly to provide for us, so finding the extra time to juggle our extracurricular activities was especially challenging. It would have made sense for them to try and consolidate our activities to conserve time and energy. But they didn't. They encouraged us to pursue our individual passions. I loved dance—and still do. All of my siblings danced, but each of us had our own thing outside of dance. Mine was cheerleading.

That encouragement from my mom and dad to follow our passion was important from an early age. But the quiet gravitational pull of *instead* doing what was expected by others was still something I struggled with growing up.

One of the clearest examples of where I got it wrong was law school. But we'll get to that in a minute. First, let me give you an example of someone who stayed true to themselves: Wesley Britt.

It was the spring of 2003 amid a turbulent period for the University of Alabama's football program—Wesley had taken a redshirt season his freshman year and was now heading into his junior season playing offensive line for the Crimson Tide. He had just earned first-team All-SEC honors the previous season—his sophomore year of eligibility.

That April, he received news of an even more exclusive accolade, at least by the world's standards. He had been named as one of 22 players nationwide to the *Playboy* magazine preseason All-America team.

His initial reaction was excitement. After two seasons as a starter for the Tide, he was being recognized as one of the very best players in the country. That was a big deal, especially for someone his age.

The honor also came along with another perk—a week in California with the other 21 players. However, there was a catch—part of the trip would include a photo shoot of the players for inclusion in the magazine.

Now, let's be honest—most college-age men in his position would have jumped at that opportunity. Both the tribute and the once-in-a-lifetime revelry and recognition. And he was getting a lot of peer pressure to not pass it up.

But it was against Wesley's beliefs, both religiously and morally. As he began to think about it, he grew uncomfortable.

"I spend a lot of time with kids, speaking to church groups and to schools, and I just don't think this would be setting a good example," Wesley told his hometown newspaper at the time.

Then, God sent him a clear sign.

When the magazine followed up with the exact date of the photo shoot, Wesley immediately realized he had a prior commitment that very day. As the Lord would have it, Wesley was already scheduled to speak to the youth group at his home church, First Baptist Church in Cullman.

Talk about God putting things in clear perspective for us. There is no doubt that God challenges us to do the right thing, but He also puts up guardrails to help us stay true to His plan.

Wesley couldn't fathom calling his pastor to say he had to back out of speaking about the Word to go appear in *Playboy*. He also thought and prayed about how his decision would impact his long-term ability to be a disciple and advance the kingdom of God.

"But after thinking about it for a while, I decided this is not one of my goals," he added at the time. "I put God first, and I set my goals for Him. I talked to God about it, and I felt it just wasn't the right thing to do."

It wasn't what he wanted. He didn't care that it was what people expected or that he was passing up a cool opportunity. He stood strong and did the hard thing—the right thing. He publicly declined the accolade and the trip.

Now, the way I learned this lesson is a different story.

I was enrolled as a 1L student at the University of Alabama School of Law in the fall of 2010, five years after I completed my undergraduate degree in Tuscaloosa. Wesley and I had recently moved back to Alabama from New England, after he retired from the NFL. Ridgeway was a newborn and Bennett was just a year old. Wesley was going back to school himself to pursue his MBA—that's what he wanted to do to launch his post-playing career in business. He wanted people to know he was more than an athlete—and he certainly accomplished that, ultimately finishing at the top of his MBA class.

I went back to law school, but not really because I wanted to practice law. It was what I felt like was long expected of me. I had previously promised my dad I would do it. And, with two little ones to care and provide for, I needed a plan and candidly could not come up with a better one.

After my freshman year of college, when I realized that the

path of medical school and becoming a doctor wasn't my calling, I ultimately changed my major to political science and became set on going to law school. Even at that time, I did not have any burning desire to practice law. That wasn't what I wanted. Looking back, I felt like the world expected me to get some kind of advanced degree, so when medical school no longer appealed to me, law school seemed like a natural alternative. As a girl, I never dreamed of becoming an attorney. It was that growing up, society told us that it was prestigious to have letters behind your name, whether it be MD or JD. That degree was a sign of intellect and of accomplishment and of stature, or so we were taught. It was expected of me that I *become someone.* For whatever reason, it seemed that an advanced degree would accomplish that. So, for a time, I lost sight of *being me.*

After undergrad, I went to work for Senator Shelby as his deputy press secretary in Washington, DC. That's what I wanted to do, as government service had become my passion through Girls State, SGA, and then my collegiate internship with Senator Shelby. I told my parents that I would go to law school eventually. They worried that I would get sucked into politics and that I would never fulfill that pledge.

So, the time came near the end of my first year working in Senator Shelby's office. I told him that I was headed back to Tuscaloosa for law school. He asked me to stay a little longer and run his press shop. I was only 23 years old, and I didn't think I was ready for that big of a role.

I remember telling him at the time, "Sir, you pay me to tell you when you have a bad idea. Well, putting me in charge of *all* of this, that's a bad idea."

Luckily, he won out in that conversation, and I stayed a little longer. Little did I know at the time that his wife, Dr. Annette Shelby, had encouraged him to give me the chance. That additional experience was a game changer for me, enhancing my professional exposure, understanding, and skill sets.

I then returned to Tuscaloosa after three years in Senator Shelby's office, but not to law school. I took a job working for Dr. Robert Witt, President of the University of Alabama. His first year leading the University came during my SGA presidency, so we had worked together on key issues facing campus and the student body. Again, I was passionate about this service. So, the job was something I wanted to do—identifying problems and creating substantive, tangible solutions. I thought I could make a real positive difference and do what I enjoyed, all while working for one of my mentors. I knew the difference my college experience made for me, and I wanted an opportunity to help create that for someone else.

My next move was to New England when Wesley and I got married. He was playing for the Patriots at the time. I packed up from Tuscaloosa and headed north. That's what I wanted—to be with my best friend and partner in life. What was expected of me took a back seat, as it should have.

But when I got to Foxboro, I was soon lost. I was providing support for Wesley, which was an important role, but I never figured out how to make room for truly pursuing my purpose. There was a burning desire in me to do something, to help people, to be a part of the solution, but I didn't know how that would work.

When the Foxboro chapter in our life came to an end, I still hadn't gotten a fancy degree or landed some lofty job. I was stuck in a mode of not prioritizing my calling. I was going with the flow and doing what was expected of me. So, law school it was. It was time to keep my word to my parents. And, even though I still did not want to practice law, I thought the degree itself would open doors in the future—it could be helpful in a small business practice or a myriad of other uses outside the courtroom.

Now, I've had a lot of bad ideas in my life. But heading to law school with two babies, while Wesley was in graduate school, might just take the cake.

That was certainly a hard thing. Being a wife and taking care of my children came first. So, studying came second. I would do my coursework whenever I could spare a moment. While they were napping. After they ate. After I tried putting them to bed. In between them waking up in the middle of the night. First thing in the morning before I took them to daycare.

Sometimes, the multitasking had to enter the classroom. When one of my children was sick, daycare couldn't let them stay. And I couldn't miss class. So, I would take them to school with me. I remember being in Torts class with Ridgeway at six months old. It was a large lecture-style classroom. I set up a blanket on the ground right beside me, underneath the tabletop, and that's where Ridgeway laid all class. People could hear him but not see him. I could really only hope he wouldn't make much noise. It helped having a professor who just rolled with it (thank you, Professor Lyons!).

Most students were traditional in the sense that they entered law school right after undergrad. I was a handful of years older than the majority of my peers, I was married, and I had two young children. One day, I remember being in a study group where everyone else was talking about being in middle school during the Y2K scare, a stark contrast from me remembering it as a senior in high school. Don't get me wrong—I made some of my lifetime best friends in law school that I still cherish to this day. But boy, did I feel old at the time.

Law school on its face plus the challenges of being a wife and a good momma to two little ones simultaneously was already undoubtedly *tough enough*. However, on April 27, 2011, the day before our spring final exams were to begin, when our home and car were destroyed and most of our possessions were lost in the EF4 tornado that hit Tuscaloosa, the *tough enough* became almost unbearable.

The rest of campus besides the law school canceled finals for the spring after the devastation of April 27. The law school simply pushed them back a little bit. Thankfully, they gave me a little extra time than that due to our family's extraordinary circumstances. Still, amid everything else I had to get my head and my arms around in the following days, I had to forge ahead with—and, in a way, restart—cramming for exams.

Besides the time crunch and the mayhem in which I found myself, my notes, textbooks, and classwork from the semester were lost in the tornado. I tried to muster the ability to make light of the situation, joking that hopefully Dorothy made good use of them at the school of law in Oz.

The incredible truth is that some of our possessions had flown across the state of Alabama. A photo of me as a teenager and two friends whom I danced with was found in Rainbow City, Alabama—more than 100 miles away from Tuscaloosa. We only learned of its whereabouts and retrieved it when the person who found it posted it on Facebook asking for help identifying someone in the photo. "That's a young Katie Boyd Britt," a mutual friend said, tagging me in the post.

What a surreal moment. But it wasn't the only one. A good Samaritan found our family checkbook. Again, it had traveled halfway across the state, counties away from Tuscaloosa. Not only did they mail it back to us, but they slipped in a $20 bill with a note that contained kind words hoping that we were safe and healthy and encouraging us. If that gesture of simple goodness from a complete stranger doesn't define Alabama, I don't know what does.

Some of our possessions flew shorter distances. For blocks around our house, people reported finding Wesley Britt bobbleheads after April 27. Sometime after his playing days on campus, the University's athletic department had notified Wesley that they had found an extra box of these classic promotional items, featuring him in his #70 Crimson Tide jersey. They were kind enough to give us this box, which was sitting in our attic when disaster struck. Some of the bobbleheads somehow survived the storm—we actually gave some away 10 years later when I was on the campaign trail. But many of them were not so lucky. Bobbleheads showed up in people's yards and on the street after being flung around town by the tornado. A few were still intact, yet many lost their heads. That was another reminder—a bizarre one—of how fortunate we were to be alive.

There is a less morbid story of where some of our possessions ended up in Tuscaloosa. Wesley was in the Bryant Museum, which chronicles the history of the University of Alabama football program, on campus in 2012 for a function honoring former players. During the event, he came across an exhibit he had never seen—it focused on April 27, 2011's impact on the city. As he examined the display, something special caught his eye: an autographed football that had been found in the aftermath of that day. It was Wesley's football. He had the tradition going back to high school of getting all of his teammates to sign a ball every season. This one, which he thought until that moment was gone for good, was from the 2002 season with the Tide. He asked the museum's director about the ball. It was found in a driveway miles away from our house.

Even more incredibly, it was found by the late, legendary Tuscaloosa sportswriter, Cecil Hurt. Cecil had no way at the time to know whom the ball belonged to, so he donated it to the museum for the exhibit. Once Wesley made the discovery that it was his, the museum of course offered to return it immediately. Wesley allowed it to remain on display for years afterward. The ball would finally make its long-awaited return home to us in 2018.

That was certainly an outlier, however. Most of our possessions were gone with the wind on April 27, 2011. I remember crawling on my hands and knees amid the wreckage, trying to find some kind of memento of our children's first moments on earth, like the little bracelets they wore at the hospital. Most of our family memorabilia was lost. My own school yearbooks and many of my pictures from growing up were lost permanently. Little moments captured on paper, notebooks, and the like were no more. Even the backup electronic storage drive—where I thought our memories would be safe forever—was gone, taking with it precious pictures of family moments that we can never get back.

And then, there were all my class materials, which were unimportant in the grand scheme of what we had lost but were rather urgent from a timeliness perspective.

My notes were copious, and all the materials were prepped just how I liked them. My books were tabbed. Documents were highlighted just so. Key points were arranged in a precise manner to fit how I learn information. I had worked nearly all semester on them.

Thankfully, the law school gave me a new textbook and allowed me someone else's outline to study from. These notes were solid, but they weren't *mine*. Learning the format of the materials and finding everything I needed again was a process in itself. I essentially had to start studying all over again.

Given the circumstances, my exam deadline was pushed back, for which I was grateful. Yet, I had a few other things going on at the same time.

I began my first summer associate position in early May at a well-respected law firm in Birmingham. And this is really where my doing what was expected instead of what I wanted reached another level.

I worked hard in law school to land competitive summer positions because I thought that's what I was supposed to do. In my head, you were not successful as a law student unless you were offered associate opportunities with the big firms—the *good* ones. The truth is that I lacked the courage to chart a different path even though I knew in my gut that I wasn't meant to practice law and that my future should not be in a courtroom. I was too afraid to do something different. Better yet, I didn't know what else to do.

I had a one-year-old and a two-year-old, our house was gone, I only had a borrowed car, and I still had to take my final exams. Another layer of challenge was added for the first half of the summer—Wesley, as a part of his MBA program, headed to a foreign country to study abroad. He offered to cancel his trip after the tornado hit, but I insisted he go in order to not disrupt his education. That's what he wanted to do, and it was important to me that he not be deprived of his opportunity.

What an adventure that summer turned out to be.

Every day consisted of driving back and forth from Tuscaloosa to Birmingham along Interstate 59. It was about an hour each way. Each morning, I had to find someone to drop my children off at daycare, because I had to be at the law firm before daycare opened. The drive time would consist of me trying to work the phone, trying to regroup and recover from our lives being upended on April 27. I was gathering information for our insurance claims and making lists of things we needed, which included everything from a new car to baby Tylenol. After driving back to Tuscaloosa in the evening, I would pick up the children and go into full mom mode. It was time for dinner. Then it was playtime. One silver lining was that Bennett and Ridgeway had more toys at this time than they did before the tornado. Once friends and family members heard their toys were lost in the storm, people came out of the woodwork to offer up their previously used baby toys. We still did not know what insurance would cover, and money was tight enough just trying to replace the essentials like diapers and clothes, so people's generosity meant more than words can express.

After playtime it was bath time. They were both at the stage of having little puffy hands—you know the kind where their little plump forearm dips down into the crease of their wrist only to pop right back up—and you just want to spend all day squeezing them. Those kind of baby chunks made bath time even more of an adventure as I'd work to ensure they were actually clean. Then I would read to them both before bed. Some of their favorites were *Love You Forever*, *Brown Bear, Brown Bear, What Do You See?*, and *The Very*

Hungry Caterpillar. Pete the Cat was also a childhood favorite, but that came a little later in their toddler years.

After they went to bed, it was time to do some more insurance work, study for exams, and try to finish whatever work I hadn't completed that day at the law firm.

At some point, there came a little sleep.

Some people were more gracious about the situation than others. My sister Jackson was living in Tuscaloosa at the time and was a huge help through all of this. Then, there was the opposite side of the coin. I remember telling a partner at one of the firms at which I was a summer associate that I needed to leave about 40 minutes early one afternoon in order to get home to get our air conditioner fixed. I explained to him that I didn't want my babies having to try to sleep through another night in the blazing Alabama summer heat. He reacted by asking, "Isn't there someone else who could do that for you?"

No. There was *not.*

That was a lesson in its own right. After that day, I've tried to be mindful that people are all going through different seasons in life, and that we should each be intentional and gracious in how we respond when someone acknowledges a challenging situation they are facing. But that summer yielded other lessons, too.

A stretch that May was particularly brutal. One night, after doing all the mom things and getting the children to bed, I took a final exam from 1:00 to 4:00 a.m. I then slept for a solid hour, got everyone up and headed to daycare, drove to Birmingham, and then drove to Anniston with the firm for a deposition. All those final exams were hard things. They went well overall, but I will always be most proud of my A+ on that middle-of-the-night Contracts exam.

But the being you part—I wasn't so proud of that, because that part of me was missing in action. I was trying to be everything everyone else wanted me to be, but I was not truly following the Lord's plan for me. Much of that was needed, of course. But I was leaving no room for me to process what we had been through. I was just getting through the day.

COMPARISON CAN BE CANCEROUS

In the book of our own life, if there's a story we want written, we have to be the one to write it. We have to pick up the pen, have the courage to title the chapter, and be willing to do what it takes to write the words.

I knew that practicing law wasn't what I wanted my life's pages to hold. But I was insecure, and I wasn't sure what else I could do. I was too worried about what others expected of me—I lost sight of what I truly wanted. I lost sight of pursuing my passion and my calling.

And ultimately, I conformed. I sought a summer associate position because that's what other people do—and what other people defined as success. I thought that if I didn't get a clerkship, people would think that I had failed. The thought of that judgment was paralyzing.

We have the tendency to do this throughout life, and it can really hold us back.

We do it with relationships of all kinds—professional relationships, classmates, friendships, and even with people we barely know. We feel the silent pull to conform to their definition of success instead of our own. We end up leaning into what they like or how they act, versus focusing on who we are.

Even when we are not conforming, we are comparing ourselves to others. This "compare and despair" can be equally as or even more unhealthy.

From an early age, my parents encouraged me to be *my* best—not necessarily *the* best. There is a big difference. In the first case, the measuring stick is about *you*. In the second, the measuring stick is about *others*.

Two distinct memories from my childhood illustrate this point.

I was on the varsity cheerleading squad starting my 10th grade year at Enterprise High School—my first year at the school. At practice every week, we would do a line of jumps. And my jumps were really good, particularly my toe touches. This wasn't hubris speaking—I could compare myself to the others around me, and it was clear. But my cheerleading coach would never compliment me. She complimented others, people whose jumps I knew were not better than mine. It ate me up inside. *Does she just not like me? Am I doing something wrong?*

I finally asked my mom about it one day. I'll never forget how easily she analyzed the situation. "She is not going to compliment you for being *the* best. She will compliment you when she knows you're giving *your* best. Those are two different things," my mom advised. Lightbulb moment! She was right.

My coach was doing me a huge favor the entire time; I just didn't realize it until then. I worked harder and harder to be my best—and to elevate the ceiling of what my best could be. That taught me self-discipline and to be motivated by my desire to be better instead of the world fluffing my ego.

Another memory, again involving my mom keeping it real with me: When I was in eighth grade, we traveled to Atlanta to compete in the regional Teen Miss Dance, a competition hosted by Dance Masters of America. Our region consisted of Alabama, Tennessee, and Georgia. The competition was held at a hotel with a huge, classic atrium. I remember the hotel was connected to a mall, where there was a Ruby Tuesday. That might have been what I was looking forward to most about the weekend. Ruby Tuesday hadn't made its way to the Wiregrass yet, so it was fine dining to me. I could have eaten my weight in that brown bread, covered thickly in a spread of honey butter.

I ended up winning the competition and advancing to Teen Miss Dance of America.

But the first thing my mom told me after I stepped off that stage in Atlanta was that I didn't deserve to win. She explained—directly but kindly—that she knew leading up to the competition I had not prepared like I should have and like I was capable of. She told me calmly but plainly that I had not been *my* best that night during the performance itself—and, in fact, she also believed that I was not *the* best either on the day. She did not mince her words when she said that Leah, one of my dearest friends, worked harder than me, performed better than me, and deserved to take home the trophy instead of me.

I still think about that. I never want a victory that I didn't earn. I continue to think back, "Could I have practiced harder? Prepared more? Put in more work before hand?" The truth is yes. And measuring and evaluating yourself that way is how you get better.

That night taught me another lesson—that winning doesn't feel nearly as good if ultimately you don't believe that you deserve it. I never wanted to feel like that again. And that is why my mentality to this day is to always give it my best and leave it all on the field. That night also made it clear that even on the days that you achieve "success," there may be someone else in the room that deserves it more. Appreciating the talent, sacrifices, and hard work of others—not just your own—is critical to growth, humility, and the path to being your best.

The concept of focusing on how you can be *your* best, not focusing on whether or not you are *the* best, is easier said than done. Remember, we naturally tend to look at the person next to us and compare ourselves to them. We do it without even meaning to do it. We do it without thinking of doing it.

Many times, this leads to us fixating on the other person's strength and our comparative lack of ability in that area, instead of looking at the strength we bring to the table or something that uniquely sets us apart.

We have to realize that God made us all different for a reason. It's constructive to be self-aware and work to improve areas in which we are weak, but we shouldn't obsess over that area being someone else's strength.

Be your own measuring stick.

Comparing ourselves to other people is the ultimate trap. The social media age has made this even worse across every facet of modern life. But this negative dynamic predates the online revolution. For generations, people have fallen prey to compare and despair. Whether it's on your phone, at home, in the classroom, or in the boardroom, here's my best advice: God made you unique—one of a kind—so focus on *you*. Your passions. Your strengths. Your talents.

Never forget that what you can contribute is different from any other person on this planet.

That's something I have had to remind myself of throughout life. It's a constant internal dialogue.

Is what I bring to the table good enough? Am I good enough? I find myself asking. I think we all face the same persistent doubt from time to time.

Throughout high school and college, I fell into the trap of comparing myself to others. On paper, I seemed to never have as much when I played that game. There was the girl in Junior Miss who had a 36 on the ACT. There was the girl at Girls State whose mom was a judge. The guy involved on campus at the University of Alabama whose dad was a trustee. A sorority sister whose mom was president of the sorority back in her collegiate days. How could I measure up to these things?

The moment you start letting those doubts get in your head is the moment you start to lose. Keep your eyes on the Lord and be confident in Him that being *you* is enough. *You* are enough.

To this day, I still have to tell myself to remember that.

I think back to a time in the summer of 2022. It was after I won the tough primary and primary runoff races for the US Senate. I was the Republican nominee in Alabama and was attending a fundraiser in Texas with some fellow GOP Senate nominees from across the nation.

I made the mistake of looking around and comparing myself to the others in the room. Internally, I was using them as a measuring stick as I asked the question, *Am I good enough?*

It seemed like they all went to Ivy League schools. And their professional accomplishments—wow. Venture capitalist. Best-selling author. Sitting congressman. Renowned doctor and talk show host. Son of a former US Senator. I started thinking about what I *didn't* bring to the table, versus what I actually did bring.

I hoped that during the remarks portion I would be called on last to at least give me a chance to hear these guys speak first. I hoped that I could offer something comparable, that I wouldn't seem out of place or, even worse, out of my league. As usual, I had excused myself from the room before remarks to say a prayer, asking God to guide me. No matter how inconsequential the moment may seem, I want to ask Him to walk with me.

When I returned, I was internally giving myself a pep-talk that I didn't have to be *them*, I just had to be *me*. And ultimately, I needed to own being me. I am proud of where I'm from and where I was educated, how I was raised and the values that are important to me. By worldly standards my résumé might not stack up, but I reminded myself that doesn't make me any less worthy of being in the room. I was letting my own insecurities get in the way of God's purpose for me.

There are certainly situations where the world places limitations on us, but I have found that it is the ones we place on ourselves that actually do the most damage. Don't let your own insecurities limit your potential. Remember that God has a purpose and a path for you, and you just have to have the courage to walk it.

Whenever you find yourself in a similar situation and you are questioning your worthiness or ability to belong, remember what Ephesians 2:10 tells us.

For we are his workmanship, created in Christ Jesus for good works, which God prepared beforehand, that we should walk in them.

God has a plan for each and every one of us. And we will never reach our full potential trying to be anyone but ourselves. So, use the gifts that God has given you and truly be *you*.

CHAPTER 4

Keep Being You, Even When It's Hard

THIS WAS A LESSON that was particularly hard for me to learn, starting in eighth grade.

That's when the bullying began. We didn't even really call it that back then. I just thought of it as kids being mean.

In movies and in TV shows, we often see cheerleaders stereotyped as part of the "cool" crowd. And while many might have assumed that was the case from the outside, *well*, that wasn't me.

I loved to cheer. But socially, it was more challenging to fit in. It's not that I didn't like the other girls who cheered. In fact, I looked up to some of the older ones—including some of the ones who ended up being the ugliest to me.

I worked hard in school and took my studies very seriously. And when I wasn't dancing or cheering, my idea of a fun night out was going with friends to shop at Walmart and then heading to Shoney's afterward. Before we got our licenses, we would get my mom to drive us. I didn't drink throughout high school, and my favorite way to end any night was hearing about my friends' weeks while making chocolate chip cookies from scratch. I am fairly certain that we ate more dough than we baked, but that was part of the fun.

In many ways, I simply stuck out. In other ways, I didn't conform. And in junior high and high school, doing either is a really bold thing.

One particular in-class moment still sticks in the back of my head. It was near the end of the year in eighth grade—the time to turn in our textbooks. In one of my classes, a boy took my textbook from me, hocked a loogie in it, closed it, and handed it back to me. "Good luck with that," he said as our classmates looked on. Laughter erupted.

The bullying got worse in ninth and tenth grades.

In ninth grade, I decided to run for student council. As you know by now, it hadn't worked out well the last time I tried, but I had built up the courage to try again. We were allowed one week to campaign during which you could put up posters, hand out stickers, and make your pitch to your fellow classmates. Because there was such a limited time frame, I knew I needed to use every moment. I worked over the weekend on my posters and had scouted out the best locations to put them.

When that Monday morning rolled around, I was ready, *or so I thought*. I got to school early and went immediately through the doors on the far end of the carpool line. Those doors were closest to both halls that housed the majority of the academic classrooms, so I thought it would be the best place to start. I grabbed a poster spot close to that entrance and the main office and then took a left and headed down the long hall. There were a series of windows on one side and classrooms on the other, leaving limited wall space in a high trafficked area.

I could hear them before I could see them. Several of the most popular girls from the high school walked through the doors of Dauphin with posters in their hands. Just their sheer presence in the hallway that morning caused me to freeze in my tracks. It wasn't lost on me that high school girls would *never* be caught on a junior high campus unless it was personal. I could feel my heart beating in my throat. It was clear they not only wanted *me* to know that they wanted me to lose, they wanted to make sure the *whole school* knew it too. They were successful; word got around that morning. The posters. Their words. And ultimately when the votes were tallied, they were quick to claim a victory. I lost. But for several of them, that wasn't enough. They kept finding ways to make me feel uncomfortable in my own skin.

That year was filled with real low points. There were ridiculous rumors and unkind gestures, but the worst came that spring when school was winding down. I had recently made the cheerleading squad for my upcoming 10th-grade year—my first year of high school. Our junior high went through 9th grade and then our high school years were 10th through 12th.

I was in class when I heard my name ring out over the intercom. An envelope was delivered to the school's front office, and I was summoned to come retrieve it. I got up from my desk and made the walk down the hallway. I picked it up, said "Thank you," and stepped out of the front office to return to class. I opened it as I walked back to class. Immediately, I stopped in my tracks in the middle of the hallway, pulling it close to my body as if to ensure no one else could see it—although I was alone. I was shocked. The note inside featured a depiction of my body as looking like a man. Still to this day, I don't like to show my arms as a result. The note also said very derogatory, plainly untrue things. It was from some of those same girls. I went into the bathroom to attempt to collect myself before returning to class.

That was certainly a different day and age in how schools operate across the board. This was an era when the doors of the school were always unlocked. Email wasn't a thing so printed schedules, fundraising packets, notes, or just a dance bag you might have left home were all delivered to the office with ease and then to students with few questions asked. It was also a small town where people knew each other, and no one had reason to be suspicious of much of anything. I never asked whether those girls even gave the office a cover story of what the note was about. More likely, good intentions were simply assumed.

I can only imagine how much worse this phase of my life would have been with smartphones and social media added into the equation. Young women and young men today can't escape this kind of pressure simply by going home at the end of the day. It follows them around on their phones and other electronic devices. Kids are even more emboldened to be mean behind the anonymity and distance that social media offers. And what's said—and the pictures and the videos that are posted—are memorialized permanently online. Not even time can separate children and teenagers from what happens on social media.

Things were rough back then outside of the school walls, too. In 10th grade at Enterprise High School, I was coming home from dance one evening when I got to a cross street right up the hill from my house. A truck pulled out behind me—these kids had been waiting. I pulled into the driveway, and they pulled their truck perpendicular across the driveway entrance on the street. I could see through the mirror that in the bed of the truck was a group of the usual suspects who normally gave me a hard time at school.

I waited for what seemed like an eternity to see if they would get out—or leave. They didn't budge.

The moment I got out, they began to egg my car, our house, and me. And they did it all in front of Jackson. I begged them to at least let my little sister go inside. They laughed some more.

Looking back now, the cruelest part was that they waited for me to come home and then get out of my car to see the look of total devastation on my face as they did it.

I wanted to be strong for my sister. We came inside and told my parents. Jackson was beyond upset. She has a heart the size of Texas and keeps up a tougher exterior to protect it. If you mess with her it's one thing, but if you mess with one of her sisters—*watch out.* They talked through it with us, and then my dad went with me to drive my car to the car wash before the eggs could settle in on the paint. When Dad and I got home, I assured Jackson I was fine and not to give it another thought. I went and found Mom later that night to discuss it again once Jackson had gone to bed. This just felt different because my little sister now had to experience it. That made me more upset than usual. My mother quickly reminded me *who* I was and *whose* I was. And that neither anger, resentment, or bitterness were productive long-term.

She constantly turned me to the clear and powerful words of Romans 12:17-21, over and over again.

Do not repay evil for evil. Be careful to do what is right in the eyes of the everyone. If it is possible, as far as it depends on you, live at peace with everyone. Do not take revenge, my dear friends, but leave room for God's wrath, for it is written: "It is mine to avenge; I will repay," says the Lord. On the contrary: "If your enemy is hungry, feed him; if he is thirsty, give him something to drink. In doing this, you will heap burning coals on his head." Do not be overcome by evil, but overcome evil with good.

She would follow up by reiterating the words and reminding me that vengeance is not ours and that we are not to repay evil with evil. But instead, we are called to do a hard thing—show kindness in the face of it. Then she would make me reread the last verse—do not be overcome by evil, but overcome evil with good. She worked diligently to instill in me *that* was the path the Lord was directing me to take.

I had a similar experience on a separate occasion and clung to the words and verses my mother had so often shared with me. One night I got behind the wheel of her hunter green Dodge Neon sedan, with two of my best friends riding along. We had been invited to a party on someone's farmland. When we pulled down the dirt road to where we were supposed to be, it became crystal clear—it was an ambush. People came out from every nook and cranny, eggs in hand. They waited until we opened the doors, and then they started egging us and the car. There was no party. We were the entertainment.

It was humiliating for me—I was the target, while my friends were only in the line of fire because they were with me. I felt guilty that they ended up in that position just because they were my friends, which was nothing new for them *unfortunately*. But I also appreciated it more than they knew. They were true friends, as their actions evidenced. They didn't follow the crowd. They stood by me, even though it was unpopular—even though it was hard. The easier thing would have been to pick up an egg carton and join in.

Showing kindness to someone in the little, everyday moments of life can make a huge, lasting difference. It takes real strength to do what my friends did. They stood for someone else—and for something, as a result—even when it made their own lives uncomfortable.

We need more people to do hard things like that. The world would be a much better place if we would all focus on helping bring more people into the fold rather than keeping people down who are already struggling or out of place.

Most of the people who treated me so unkindly when we were younger have apologized since then. I had long moved on and didn't hold a grudge. Look, we all make mistakes when we're young. We handle things immaturely, because we're immature—and I recognized that. But it was still like a weight off of my shoulders—a weight I didn't realize was there—when I got those apologies years down the road. It was liberating and brought a sense of peace that I can't quite explain. I'm grateful for those individuals who had the willingness and character to come to me and say they were sorry. Even if significant time has passed, an apology can still be powerful for both parties involved.

Unfortunately, peer pressure often causes people to become one of the gang, instead of sticking to the values that Christ taught us—and the actions that would make our families proud. Treat people with respect, and always live by the Golden Rule: treat others the way you want to be treated.

I can attest firsthand to the invisible scars that can be left on us by others when they don't follow that simple advice. Whether it be from growing up, college, my professional life, or even my US Senate campaign, I still have wounds that are not quite healed and other scars that I'm not ready to talk about. I may never be ready, and that's ok. They are *my* wounds, *my* scars, and if I choose to open them back up, it will be on *my* time.

What's scary is that it's even easier today to inflict these kinds of wounds. Social media has led to people living behind screens. Eggs have been replaced with online comments that live on for eternity. Bullies today are injected with false courage in cyber space, and they are emboldened to say things online that they would never have the nerve to say face-to-face. Kids snap a quick pic of a "friend" and then blast it off to others before thinking about the long-term implications. False narratives or unkind things are rapidly shared through group text chains of 12-year-olds, and before you know it, a child is completely isolated.

Apps that track and share your location are constantly being refreshed by our youth. There is a fear of being excluded and an automatic confirmation if you are. They can tell if all of their friends are together, making it crystal clear if they are left out. And don't worry, if they aren't tracking each other's locations on apps, there will inevitably be a picture posted of everyone together at whatever dinner, birthday party, concert, or spend the night, so you know that not only were you not included, but you know how much fun it was as well. And why?

Let's be honest. We as adults struggle with these very things. FOMO hits us, too. Now imagine navigating the challenges of your teenage years with this technology at your fingertips. It is imperative each of us is mindful of these dynamics and intentional in guarding against it when raising our kids. Lead by example. While you certainly have the ability to post harsh or demeaning words, pile on someone via a text chain, or memorialize a fabulous invitation, I ask that you think of others. The next generation is learning from us and just because you can, doesn't mean you should. Wesley and I have told our children's teachers every year at their parent-teacher conference that while we want them to excel academically, the most important thing to us is that they are *kind*. And if and when they are not, we want to hear about it immediately.

I know what a difference kindness can make. But even with my friends' support and the support of my family, the weight of all of this was still a lot as a teenager—and that was without all the technology of today. I didn't want to go back to school. I felt so alone. My family talked through next steps. My parents were working to provide for their four girls so private school wasn't an option. They considered sending me off to another public school district in which a family friend lived, but it just seemed so far away.

I didn't want to leave my sisters. I didn't want to run away. But I didn't want to let my heart get hard.

I prayed for that very thing. That the Lord would guard my heart.

Ultimately, with God's grace and the support of loved ones, I found a way to power through it. But I did my best not to let any of the ugliness—any of the bullying—change who I was.

I was trying to be the person that I thought God called me to be. I was trying to be the daughter my parents raised me to be. I was trying to be the big sister my siblings needed me to be. And I was trying to be the friend that my friends deserved for me to be.

I was trying to be me.

It apparently wasn't popular—it seemed to make me a target of ridicule. Then again, doing what's right isn't always what's cool. Doing a good thing is often doing a hard thing. Conforming or changing would have been the easy thing. It would have made my life easier, without a doubt. But I wouldn't have been me.

Still, the experience made me grapple with the question, *Is being me good enough?*

Am I good enough?

You likely will ask yourself the same questions from time to time. Everyone does. It's human nature.

And I am here today to tell you the answer is YES.

You are good enough. You *are* enough.

I would venture to say that *you* being *you* is great.

Whenever these questions pop into your mind, remember the words from 1 Corinthians 3:16.

Do you not know that you are God's temple and that God's Spirit dwells in you?

God's spirit lives in you. He will equip you with all that you need. You are beneath no one. You are fearless. You belong.

And just a quick reminder: *being you* doesn't require what the world would call "a journey of self-discovery." Finding out who you are can be achieved by reading God's Word. If you read the Bible like God's love letter to you, then you can discover how you're made in His image. Discovering *that* identity will help you to discover what His purpose is for you.

So be you. And strive to be your best every single day.

That's how we will get back to our collective best, too. America is best only when we demand that each American is our respective best.

This is going to require a mindset shift throughout our society. We need to stop comparing ourselves to others. We need to stop using other people as measuring sticks. We need to stop trying to be others.

We need to start being ourselves again.

This can be a hard thing at times. But God made you like you for a reason. Trust in Him. Embrace being you. Have fun being you. Remain true to yourself. And let being you help you achieve your best.

Be you, knowing that God will walk with you every step of the way.

CHAPTER 5

Don't Be a Title Holder, Be a Change Agent

WHILE WE CAN NEVER FORGET who we are and whose we are, it's also imperative that we always remember our "why."

It can be easy throughout life to get caught up in the moment. We can fixate on the day-to-day so much that the bigger picture drifts out of focus. We are liable to lose sight of the forest while staring at the tree in front of us.

Don't get me wrong—the "what" is important. But over time, we will drift off course if there is not a rhyme and a reason driving our actions.

Purpose must be our starting point and our ending point. Our "why" should be our North Star, guiding our "what" every step along life's journey.

Different people have different purposes. That's how God drew it up. He gives each of us unique talents and gifts. The common denominator is that we are all called to use ours to make a difference.

Romans 12:6-8 tells us, "*We have different gifts, according to the grace given to each of us. If your gift is prophesying, then prophesy in accordance with your faith; if it is serving, then serve; if it is teaching, then teach. If it is to encourage, then give encouragement; if it is giving, then give generously; if it is to lead, do it diligently; if it is to show mercy, do it cheerfully."*

Your talents and gifts are unique, and so is your purpose. Don't shy away from your distinctive calling. Embrace it. And be intentional about advancing that purpose in every facet of your life.

This is not an easy thing. It's something about which we must be deliberate, and it's something that we need to habitualize. You can accomplish this by constantly challenging yourself to ask, "Why?"—even if you're asking yourself the question. Make it a standardized process in your life. Always ask the question as a routine, so you won't wake up one day and realize your life is rudderless, careening toward an iceberg—or lost in the middle of the ocean, with no sense of direction to find your way back to land.

Ask the question inquisitively and be open-minded throughout life. This standard practice will not only lead to increased understanding and hone your critical thinking—it will also help you stay true to your purpose. Whether you are a teenager asking your parents and your teachers, a college student asking your professors, your mentors, or your peers, a young professional asking your supervisor, your coworkers, or your colleagues, or any other season in life, ask, "Why?"

It's important to keep in mind that there are two kinds of people—title holders and change agents.

I'm here to tell you to be a change agent. Don't be a title holder.

A change agent has purpose and lives that purpose. They have a mission and calling in mind that they are working toward. A title holder, however, thinks the accomplishment is simply landing the latest line on a résumé. It's filling a piece of paper; it's checking a box. That's the end, not the means to the end, for a title holder.

A change agent knows their "why," while a title holder is stuck on their "what."

Wesley's journey to the NFL is a good starting place for understanding the difference.

He was born at Cullman Regional Medical Center and raised in Hanceville, Alabama, which is about 10 miles outside of Cullman, the seat of Cullman County. Cullman, sitting smack-dab in between Birmingham and Huntsville off of I-65, had a population of about 13,000 when Wesley was growing up. Around 18,000 residents call it home today. Cullman is now a 21st-century manufacturing hub. The city is most well-known across the Southeast for hosting Rock the South, which originated in 2012 as an intended one-year anniversary concert celebrating the local community banding together and rebuilding after the April 27, 2011, tornadoes that devastated Cullman and our state. After experiencing initial success, the concert became an annual event that benefits numerous non-profit organizations in Cullman. Rock the South's attendance blew past 100,000 in 2023 and the growth does not show signs of stopping.

Wesley is the middle child of five. He has two older sisters, Melissa and Lindsay. Then came Wesley, followed by brothers Taylor and Justin.

Hanceville is less than 15 minutes south on US-31 from Cullman. Hanceville's population swelled more than 31% when Wesley was growing up from 1990-2000, topping 2,900 residents. His mom was a teacher in Hanceville, and that's where he began his education, attending Hanceville Elementary. After his sixth-grade year, his family temporarily moved into the city limits of Cullman for about two years so they could get into Cullman's school system, which is why Wesley attended Cullman High School rather than Hanceville High School.

It's the small town, rural America culture that makes Hanceville so special to Wesley. Hearing him talk about it reminds me why I love Enterprise. It's the kind of place where everybody takes care of everybody. The community is an extension of family. And that extends to parenting. If someone else's parents saw you acting up in the Warehouse Discount Groceries in Hanceville, they'd get onto you just like you were their own child. Their church community was even more tight knit. Wesley's family attended Hanceville First Baptist Church, and he remembers that church family being as close as biological family. When they moved into Cullman's city limits, Wesley's family began attending Cullman First Baptist Church.

Thinking about growing up in Hanceville, Wesley also talks about the outdoors. He had the freedom to explore—the freedom to be a kid. He'd go out to the woods with his friends and brothers. They'd dam creeks, catch animals, and get dirty, without a care in the world. Wesley says they'd be away from the house all day until it was time to go to bed—and nobody gave it a second thought. Hanceville, to him, was a place of comfort, peace, and safety. It was home. And it was also a place in which you had the leeway to learn. You could grow by making mistakes and being better the next time as a result. Social media was not around to hold your mistakes over your head for the rest of your life. You were not penalized for being a kid. Growing pains were fleeting, not fatal. You messed up, learned your lesson, and moved on.

Hanceville is now quietly home to Our Lady of the Angels Monastery. While Wesley was growing up, the 400-acre site was a soybean farm owned by one of his best friends. Wesley recalls playing in the farm's streams and gigging frogs.

That same property now houses the Catholic Shrine of the Most Blessed Sacrament and Monastery of the Poor Clare Nuns of Perpetual Adoration. In nearby Cullman, Catholic Benedictine monks care for more than 800 acres that comprise the grounds of St. Bernard Abbey. This property distinctively houses Ave Maria Grotto, a landscaped, four-acre park in an old quarry. This garden setting features 125 miniature reproductions of some of the most famous religious structures across the globe, arranged along a serene, forested walking trail. The project was spearheaded in the early 1900s by Brother Joseph Zoetle—who was a monk at the abbey for almost 70 years—and has drawn people from around the world to Cullman for nearly 100 years now.

Food is a big part of Alabama's culture, and it was a big part of Wesley's childhood, too. The area surrounding Cullman boasts some of the best no-frills barbecue you'll ever have. Top Hat Barbecue, located just to the south of Hanceville across the county line in Blount Springs, is one of my favorite places to eat in Alabama to this day. It was one of Wesley's favorites growing up, along with Luna's Bar-B-Q in Hanceville. Each weekday, he fondly recounts walking from Hanceville Elementary School in the afternoons and past the since-closed Blue Bell factory that produced jeans and other denim products for Lee and Wrangler. That's where many of Wesley's friends' parents worked. He would keep walking to Hanceville Drug Company, where he would stop to enjoy the old-fashioned soda fountain and handspun milkshakes.

Wesley's dad was in the demolition and recycling industry, and his shop in Hanceville was in walking distance too. Wesley and his friends would walk there to borrow tools to build their clubhouses or whatever childhood project on which they were working at the time. They would bike to the nearby Walker Brothers Building Supply for materials, as well as a Snickers and a soda.

Wesley's memories of Hanceville mirror how I feel thinking back on growing up in Enterprise. I love my hometown, and I'm proud to be from there. I remember the days at Enterprise High School (*Go Wildcats!*), when I'd head to Cutts, a local meat-and-three, for lunch. Their lima beans are still my favorite. There's my favorite Mexican restaurant, Effie's, where I could practically drink the salsa with a straw. We also have a local pharmacy, Bryars-Warren, right on Main Street. As a child, I loved getting ice cream at the counter while we waited for a prescription to be filled.

Then, there were the potluck dinners—both in Enterprise and Hanceville. After church each Wednesday and Sunday, Wesley says it seemed like the whole community would gather to eat supper.

These types of meals and memories were about a lot more than food, though. They were about fellowship. That theme extended to Wesley's football days at Cullman High School, as well.

His fondest recollections center on the small-town, Friday Night Lights atmosphere that enveloped Cullman County for game days. The pageantry of it all was special. But it really boiled down to the pride Wesley felt in representing his family and his community in that uniform and on that field. It would start the night before games, when Wesley and his teammates would head to Pasquale's for pizza and no-fuss Italian fare (Fun fact—the Pasquale's in Enterprise was actually where my parents had their first date). They would hang out, break bread, and mentally prepare to step into the arena together in 24 hours' time. Friday mornings would start with breakfast at William's Barbecue. Right before each home game, the band would play the fight song as the players walked through the stands, soaking up the energy from the crowd before taking the field. Going through every bit of it, the highs and the lows, with your friends made it all worthwhile.

Wesley's parents saw from an early age the opportunities presented by his God-given size, athleticism, and abilities. They encouraged him to work hard to maximize his potential and expand what was possible for his future. The only time he missed practice was when some of his family's goats were sick and he needed to help bring them to the veterinarian. His mom was a public-school teacher, which was sacrifice enough on its own, but on top of everything else, she would drive Wesley to Birmingham every morning before school to receive extra football training. The trip was about an hour each way. They would leave around 5:00 am. Wesley still remembers physically searching for loose change to help pay for gas. The driving mileage and the personal training pushed the boundaries of what his family could afford, yet they knew it was an investment in his living his American Dream. Wesley also credits training alongside his great friend Jimmy with helping him be his best. They pushed each other to give 110% in the weight room and on the practice field, and it made both of them better.

It all paid off in the back half of his high school playing days—the time in which the collegiate recruiting process heats up. Recruiting looked a lot different back then. Now, the process is carried out largely online. Recruits build buzz and get noticed by posting workout and game film. Someone in rural Cullman County can reach any coach in the country through a computer or mobile device. However, it was another story in the late 1990s when Wesley was at Cullman High School. The internet wasn't widely used, certainly not when it came to the world of amateur athletics. That made it tougher to get noticed—harder to seek and seize opportunities. Especially in situations similar to Wesley's case. His high school had not produced a Division 1 scholarship football player in recent history, so it was not really on any collegiate program's map to begin with.

So, Wesley had to take his talents on the road and lean on his work ethic in the recruiting process. The best way to get recruited as a high school football player was the old-fashioned way—in person. To get on a collegiate program's radar, one would go to that program's camp. All the big schools had one. And that's what Wesley did. His dad not only drove him to the camps, but he also would drive Wesley's game film—physical copies on VHS—directly to coaches across the SEC. He was tireless in making sure Wesley had a chance to prove himself.

Both parents would pack up their old Suburban and take him to camps. It was the summer between his junior and senior years when he attended the University of Florida's camp in Gainesville. Steve Spurrier, "the Head Ball Coach," was leading the Gators' program at the time. The trajectory of Wesley's life changed at that camp.

Two of Wesley's friends from high school were with him, also participating in that humid central Florida summer's workouts. He recalls Coach Spurrier giving them a tour of the athletics facility. Afterward, they were riding an elevator when Coach turned to Wesley and offered him a scholarship on the spot. It was Wesley's first scholarship offer.

That moment sparked a whole new level of self-belief in Wesley.

He had already been working hard to create and seize opportunities for himself, but now he could more concretely visualize what was in the realm of possible. And it was beyond anything he could have dreamed of as a young boy in Hanceville.

Looking back all these years, Wesley says he did not foresee coming out of that Florida camp with an offer in hand. In fact, nobody really gave him a chance at all to play at any big-time DI program at that time. Little did he—or they—know what was to come. Showing up, being truly present, and leaving it all on the field combined to form the recipe for success on that occasion, he says. He doubled down on what worked for him in the weeks, months, and years to follow. That initial scholarship offer motivated him to work even harder, because he saw firsthand the fruits of his labor.

One offer soon turned into several as Wesley's rising senior summer turned to fall. News spread that Coach Spurrier was high on Wesley, and his stock began to rise as a result. Wesley also attended more camps, and programs saw up-close what Coach Spurrier saw in Gainesville.

He went to Tuscaloosa for the University of Alabama's camp. Then there was Auburn's camp. And, our family admits this begrudgingly now, the University of Tennessee's camp, where Coach Phil Fulmer had recently led the Volunteers to a national championship. These three camps each resulted in on-the-spot scholarship offers too.

At this point, Wesley's reputation preceded himself across the Southeastern Conference. Schools began to reach out and court him without even having him attend their camp.

The University of Arkansas extended him an offer out of the blue. Houston Nutt was the Razorbacks head coach at the time. Then, the University of South Carolina jumped into the mix. Lou

Holtz, formerly with Notre Dame, had recently come out of retirement to lead the Gamecocks' program. Coach Holtz actually flew to Cullman and came to Wesley's house to pitch him on joining his project in Columbia. Wesley and his parents sat in their living room as Coach Holtz tried to sell them on his program. Wesley says he remembers no more pleasant man in football than Coach Holtz, but South Carolina was not for Wesley.

Another SEC program expressed interest that did not enter into Wesley's top level of consideration.

Wesley got a cold call one day. He picked up the phone and heard the voice on the other end say, "This is Nicholas Saban with Louisiana State University."

The call did not last very long. Wesley's dad asked him who had just called.

"Some guy named Nicholas Saban. What on earth is Louisiana State University?" Wesley responded.

It soon clicked with him that "Louisiana State University" was what everyone knows simply as "LSU." But he didn't regret not further exploring Coach Saban's interest—after all, Wesley thought, that was where coaches' careers died.

Boy, was he wrong. I can't help but smile thinking about what would follow in Coach Saban's career.

Most people would not guess this now, but Wesley actually grew up as a diehard Auburn fan. Coach Tommy Tuberville, now my colleague in the Senate representing the state of Alabama, was in charge of the Tigers' program at the time. But it was members of his staff who most directly were involved in recruiting Wesley. Eddie Gran was the recruiting coordinator. But it was offensive coordinator and offensive line coach Hugh Nall whom Wesley predominantly interacted with.

All other factors aside, Wesley's heart would have been with Auburn on the Plains. However, he did not feel the love from Auburn throughout the recruitment process. Even when he received a scholarship offer ahead of his senior season, something did not quite seem right. Wesley did not feel as wanted at Auburn as he was at Florida or Alabama.

His suspicions were vindicated as his senior season got underway. Auburn pulled the scholarship offer. He could still attend and be on the roster potentially, they told him, but not on scholarship. Wesley spoke with Coach Nall, who told Wesley he would never play a snap at Auburn or in the SEC.

Fast forward a handful of years to a meeting of the Atlanta Quarterback Club. That was the first time since then when Wesley saw Coach Nall in person, besides playing against him. Coach Nall was presenting the Shug Jordan Award—named after the legendary Auburn coach—for the best offensive lineman in the SEC and the ACC. And guess what? Wesley won it.

Coach Nall was very humble and gracious about the irony of the situation. He actually brought it up on-stage to the crowd, saying that not bringing Wesley to Auburn was one of his worst recruiting mistakes. Needless to say, that was a fulfilling moment for Wesley.

But rewind back to his senior year of high school, and the scholarship rescission was a motivator then, too. Wesley took the snub and the doubt, and he used the resulting feeling as fuel. It made him want to prove Coach Nall's words wrong.

Every morning waking up at 5:00 am to go to his new local

trainer, Steve, that senior season of high school. Every time in the following offseason when it felt like a 110-degree temperature, and he'd already lost 15 pounds during practice that day. Every day, those words pushed Wesley to keep going—to dig down deep inside himself to extract every last bit of effort. Those words formed the chip on his shoulder that ultimately drove him toward greatness. To this day, Wesley says he would not have been the player he turned out to be without Coach Nall.

On the recruiting trail, Coach Spurrier and Florida never faltered. At the time, Wesley did not think that Alabama did, either. He learned differently later in life.

Coach Neil Callaway was the offensive line coach for the Tide at the time and, unbeknownst to Wesley, began to go soft on him after Auburn pulled its scholarship offer. That domino across the state almost caused Alabama to follow suit. However, Coach Dabo Swinney—who, in addition to recruiting duties, was wide receivers and tight ends coach for Alabama at the time—saw something in Wesley. And Dabo went to bat for him with the rest of the coaching staff. Dabo told them to stick with him. "This is my recruit. This is on me if it goes bad. But we're signing this guy. We want this guy."

So, Alabama stuck in there, and Wesley's choice came down to Florida and Alabama.

In early December that year, the Cullman Regional Airport was celebrating its annual Christmas party. The same day, it saw a rather public person land in hostile territory—Coach Spurrier touched down in the University of Florida's private plane, emblazoned with a big Gator head on the side.

His arrival was uneventful. The sun was still out. A small group of people greeted him outside the plane, welcomed him cordially, and asked for his autograph. Then, he drove to Wesley's house and enjoyed a great visit with the Britt family. They had dinner and spent several hours together. Meanwhile, more partygoers were arriving at the airport—and partygoers were availing themselves of spirits, and not just the Christmas variety, as the hours passed and the light faded from the sky.

By the time Coach Spurrier arrived back on the tarmac for takeoff close to midnight, the crowd, mostly comprised of Alabama fans in that part of the state, was quite rambunctious. They were also riding a high of Alabama coming off of two recent high-profile wins against Spurrier's Gators. In October of that year, the Tide had travelled to the Swamp and snapped Florida's 30-game home winning streak in an upset victory. The 40-39 overtime thriller turned out to be one of the games of the decade, led by characteristically stellar play by Alabama's star running back Shaun Alexander. Then, in the SEC Championship just days before Coach Spurrier's visit to Cullman, Alabama trounced Florida 34-7 to earn an Orange Bowl invitation.

"Coach, can you give us a, 'Roll Tide'?" some hecklers began pestering Spurrier as he walked past the crowd toward his plane ride back to Gainesville. "Coach, throw that visor down for us, just one time. Where's your headset now, Coach?"

Coach Spurrier finally reached the steps of the plane and said his final goodbyes to Wesley, his family, and the Cullman High School staff who helped host him.

One more shout came in before he could finish the journey up the steps. "Come on Ball Coach, give us a Roll Tide and throw that visor down."

Coach Spurrier apparently had reached his limits. He turned and responded.

"Yeah, you like me this year, but what about the last 10 years when I've been kicking your ass?"

Wesley still gets a chuckle out of retelling that story.

But in the moment, he was really torn between Gainesville and Tuscaloosa. He was a big fan of Coach Spurrier, and it meant a great deal to him that Florida had been the first one to offer him a scholarship. Another factor, this one in Alabama's favor, was that the Crimson Tide had a strong Fellowship of Christian Athletes chapter on campus and featured that faith focus in their recruiting efforts.

Wesley prayed for guidance, which soon came through a conversation with his grandfather.

"If you want to be Wesley Britt from Florida, do business in Florida, and raise your family in Florida, go to Florida. If you want to be Wesley Britt from the great state of Alabama, do business in Alabama, and raise your family in Alabama, go to Alabama," his grandfather told him.

His decision was made. He did not want to end up in Florida for the long run. So, he committed more than his football career to Alabama.

Wesley's first call was to Coach Spurrier. It was Christmas Eve. Wesley expressed his gratitude but told him he would be taking his talents to Tuscaloosa.

"Wes, I'm going to tell you, I thought you had more class than that," Coach Spurrier ribbed him.

While the conversation was friendly, even in that moment, the Head Ball Coach had to get in the last word.

Next, he dialed up Dabo and told him the good news. Wesley was committing to Alabama.

He made it official with a small ceremony on Signing Day in the lunchroom at Cullman High School. It was not the huge productions you see from major signees today. But his parents and high school coaches joined him (along with his best friend Jimmy, who was signing for Auburn, and his parents), the local newspapers took some photos, and that was that.

FROM CULLMAN TO THE CAPSTONE

Wesley went into his collegiate career as part of the nation's third highest ranked recruiting class. The team had just won the SEC Championship. And preseason rankings rated them as one of the best three teams in the nation. Needless to say, expectations were high for Coach Mike DuBose's 2000 team. The players had championships on their mind.

Wesley also had high expectations on a personal level. He went in thinking he would start from the beginning. Training camp, he says, was phenomenal under Coach DuBose. They had three-a-days in full pads, and it was truly grueling. This was before the rules were changed to restrict training to two-a-days—and eventually just one practice per day—and then no back-to-back full-pad practices. Times have definitely changed. Wesley can still feel the full body cramps every day after those practices. It was hard. He made it through but ended up being the backup to begin the season at both left and right tackles.

The season kicked off in Pasadena, California, against UCLA. It was Alabama's first trip to the Rose Bowl in nearly 55 years. The Bruins were coming off of a 4-7 season. The Tide was rolling into the game with a lofty preseason ranking and even grander goals for the year.

The game's opening sequences played into these expectations. UCLA punted on its opening drive, and Alabama's Freddie Milons took the punt back for a 71-yard touchdown. Wesley remembers the feeling being palpable on the sideline in that moment—this team was going to compete for a national championship.

The game quickly went downhill, as did the season. UCLA won decisively, and Alabama proceeded to post a 3-8 overall record for the season. The coaching staff considered starting Wesley throughout the first half of the season, but Coach Callaway did not want to waste his redshirt on a losing cause. Wesley ended up being grateful that was the case.

Coach DuBose left the program at the end of the season, which concluded with one of the worst records in program history. Wesley was penciled in to be a starter the coming season, but newly hired Coach Dennis Franchione wiped the slate and the depth chart clean when he arrived in town as the head coach. Coach Franchione brought in a talented junior college transfer at Wesley's position and slotted him above Wesley heading into spring camp. Wesley did not let it deter him. He worked harder than ever, although he remained the backup on the depth chart all of spring training. He did whatever he could to improve and show what he was capable of. He showed up early and put in extra work. He grinded, leaving it all on the field every day at practice. His mentality was simple—he simply needed to beat the guy in front of him.

It was not until summer training camp that Wesley found out he had done just that. He was now the starter at left tackle heading into the 2001 season—his redshirt freshman year.

That season was a good one for him personally and the team improved significantly on the prior year. Wesley ended the season being named to both the Freshman All-SEC Team and the Freshman All-America Team. The Tide went 7-5 and won the Independence Bowl to close out the season. Things were looking good heading into the 2002 season with Coach Franchione still at the helm.

However, misfortune struck the team on February 2, 2002—four days before National Signing Day. The NCAA hit Alabama football with five years of probation, including a two-year postseason ban and heavy scholarship reductions. The alleged violations stemmed from before Wesley's time on campus—and before Coach Franchione's. The present-day team was being punished for something over which it had no control.

That stung immediately. The 2002 season saw Alabama go a strong 10-3, with close losses to No. 2 Oklahoma, No. 7 Georgia, and rival Auburn in the Iron Bowl. The Tide finished atop the SEC West; however, the NCAA sanctions barred them from competing for the SEC Championship. Although the team was banned from participating in a bowl game, Alabama athletic director Mal Moore intentionally scheduled a final "regular season" game at Hawaii—with the Tide heading to Honolulu before earning a No. 11 ranking in the final Associated Press poll. Wesley was named All-SEC First Team for that redshirt sophomore season.

He soon learned another hard life lesson. Coach Franchione had rallied the team ahead of this successful season by calling on each and every player to hold his piece of the rope. The players literally held a rope as a team, with each individual then cutting off their respective piece. The pieces were then displayed above players' lockers to remind them of their responsibilities to themselves and their teammates.

The players held up their end of the bargain to the end. But Coach Franchione let go of the rope.

On the trip to Hawaii, rumors began to bubble up that Coach Franchione was not content in Tuscaloosa. However, on the return flight to Alabama, he assured Wesley and other team leaders to their face that he was not going anywhere. This was his team, he said.

Wesley never saw Coach Franchione again.

Coach Moore, the athletic director, came into the locker room the day after the team returned to town. It was early December of 2002. Coach Franchione was leaving immediately. He was going to be the head coach at Texas A&M. He had not told the team—and he would not be speaking to the team directly.

"He was still in the football facility at that very minute but could not even be bothered to share the news of his own departure," Wesley remembers.

Despite the facts of the situation and the rightful sense of betrayal the team felt, Coach Moore handled the talk with the players with the utmost class. He said that Coach Franchione was trying to do what was best for his family. "Coach Franchione loves all of you," Coach Moore said.

The next Alabama head coach was Mike Price. Wesley remembers him as a ball of energy from day one. Coach Price brought in a pocket full of sugar packets and started throwing them out to the players. "We're going to the Sugar Bowl. We're going to the National Championship," Price exclaimed. The players ate it up. They were re-energized. Spring training was perfect, Wesley recalls. Things were on the upswing. Until the next crash back down to earth.

Coach Price was fired in May 2003, before even getting to summer camp and months before what would have been his first game leading the Crimson Tide. Off-the-field decision-making ruined what his players thought could have been a good run in Tuscaloosa for Price.

This is when Wesley really took an outsized leadership role on the team. At this point, he and his teammates not only knew that they'd be unable to play for a championship or in a bowl game again in the coming season, but now they would be on their third head coach in six months. Players were granted the option to transfer to another school without having to sit out a year. It was essentially the transfer portal before the transfer portal existed.

Wesley knew the program was at a tipping point. A mass exodus could have set the program back a decade. To him, Alabama football was staring down the barrel of irreparable damage. Together with the likes of Brodie Croyle and Shaud Williams, Wesley stood in the gap and helped rally his teammates to stay together and forge ahead. Miraculously, not a single player transferred.

Wesley proved that being a leader is more than a line on a résumé—it's about much more than a title. Being a leader means you have the responsibility to do hard things.

Coach Moore hired Mike Shula, a former Alabama quarterback and son of coaching legend Don Shula, to be the Tide's new head coach. He was Wesley's fourth head coach on campus.

Wesley went into his redshirt junior season as a pre-season All-America and All-SEC honoree. Expectations were high. There was a buzz he might leave for the NFL if the year went to plan.

Although the team was struggling, Wesley was having a great individual year through eight games. Then came the Third Saturday in October—the annual rivalry game against Tennessee.

It was October 25, 2003, in Tuscaloosa's Bryant-Denny Stadium. On the sixth play of the game, Wesley's stellar season came to an abrupt end. Shaud Williams was running off of Wesley's back. The defensive end pinched inside while the linebacker dove at Shaud but got the back of Wesley's legs. He felt both bones snap in his left leg—his tibia and fibula were broken. What happened next will forever live in Alabama football lore.

"I remember Coach Shula came out on the field and expressed his sorrow for me," Wesley recalls. "I said, 'Coach Shula, I'm blessed. Even if I never set foot on this field again, just the fact that I came here, got to play at Bryant-Denny Stadium, am attending the University of Alabama, and got to meet people like you, I am nothing but blessed to have these opportunities.'"

Wesley didn't bemoan the injury. He didn't even think of himself. His attention immediately turned to helping his teammates. He told them not to worry about his injury—focus on executing your respective responsibility and winning the game, he said as he was lifted onto a stretcher. Pointing vigorously, he exhorted his teammates on the sidelines to get his message across far and wide.

Then, his attention turned to the crowd. It was not just his teammates who needed a lift. The entire stadium was audibly downtrodden. A hush had come over the crowd. Not only was the season already not working out, but now one of the Tide's star players was down for likely the rest of the year. Wesley was not going to let anyone mourn his departure from the field. As he settled into place on the stretcher, he started frenetically waving his arms as to tell the crowd to turn the volume up. He then began pumping up his fist for the crowd to see and started circling it like a pom-pom before leading the home fanbase in an impromptu version of "Roll Tide Roll."

As he was carted to the tunnel, he tilted his head toward the sky and pointed upward with both hands.

"I pointed toward Heaven, because I wanted everybody to know that the Lord Jesus was my all-in-all," Wesley affirms. "I just wanted to give glory to God, and I knew He was with me."

Tens of thousands watched from the stadium. And hundreds of thousands, like me, watched on television. I was actually in Oxford, Mississippi, when he was injured. Jackson was in school at Ole Miss, and I had planned on spending the day with her. But as the stretcher headed down the tunnel in Tuscaloosa, I headed for my car. I made it to his hospital room in Birmingham before the game had concluded. The game painfully went into five overtimes. We watched the end together.

What struck me in the moment, and what Wesley still stresses about that valley in his life to this day, is that there is no use in wallowing. He was completely at peace with what happened to him. Instead of letting the setback consume him, Wesley's perspective was that he was blessed to have the opportunity to be in a position where he was playing football for the University of Alabama in the first place. Forget being injured. He was blessed. And that hadn't changed in the grand scheme of things. He knew God had a great plan. "If it was more football, that'd be fine. If it wasn't, that'd be fine, too," Wesley reflects.

He had a great plan, and Wesley put himself in His hands. Wesley dedicated himself to following His plan, whether he could see the end result or not. And he turned the adversity into an opportunity to lead by example and encourage his teammates, the fanbase, and the national TV audience.

After surgery on his leg, intensive rehab began almost immediately. He chalks up his recovery to "a lot of prayer. A lot of hard work. And a lot of support."

A key piece of support came from his mom. He was set to graduate after three and a half years in school that December, right after the injury. His initial reaction was that he could always graduate in the spring instead. But his mom wasn't having that. She drove down from Cullman County and moved in with Wesley for the rest of that fall semester. She drove him to class every day so he could stay on track to graduate in December. She would even come in at the beginning of class to help him rearrange his desk or his table so he could prop his healing leg up on something in front of him.

Wesley graduated that December. He was named an All-SEC First Team honoree, even after missing the final four games of the season. And in January, just over two months after the injury, Wesley was squatting 405 pounds again.

It was spring of 2004. The coming season, Wesley's redshirt senior year, was set to be a special one. Taylor, Wesley's brother, had joined him in Tuscaloosa starting with the 2002 season, following a transfer from UAB. Now, his youngest brother Justin was heading to Alabama as well. With Wesley at left tackle, Taylor at center, and Justin at defensive tackle, all three Britt brothers were on the same competitive team for the first time in their lives.

On top of it all, Wesley's teammates voted him as one of the permanent team captains for the year. He took the utmost pride in his leadership, and being recognized in that manner by his teammates was the greatest honor he could have imagined.

That fall, Coach Shula's second season got off to a better start, 3-0. However, Croyle, the team's talented quarterback, was injured in that third game and lost for the rest of the season. Things quickly went downhill, and the team ended with a 6-6 record. Yet, there was a silver lining at the end of the year: Wesley's second ever bowl game—the Music City Bowl in Nashville. The program's bowl ban had ended, and they had barely cleared the threshold of bowl eligibility. Wesley was announced as a College Football News All-America First Team honoree, an AP All-America Third Team honoree, and an All-SEC First Team honoree (that one for the third time in his career), and he was named as the recipient of the prestigious Jacobs Award, which is given annually to the conference's top blocker as voted on by the coaches around the SEC.

The next bowl he played in was the Senior Bowl in Mobile, Alabama. He was receiving significant NFL interest heading into the January showcase event. Then, he suffered a hairline fracture in his right fibula while practicing at Ladd-Peebles Stadium ahead of the game. This meant he missed the NFL Combine in February as he rehabbed his leg for the next couple of months.

He was drafted by the San Diego Chargers that April and turned in a strong performance during preseason games in the following months. However, the Chargers were heavy on offensive line depth, and they let Wesley go after the final preseason contest in September.

"I know God has an awesome plan for me, and I believe everything happens for a reason," Wesley told the media at the time.

He was right. The New England Patriots immediately signed him. Wesley boarded a red-eye flight from San Diego, refocused, and counted his blessings. The resilience paid dividends. He got to learn from Coach Bill Belichick for the next four seasons. And we started our life together in Foxboro, where Bennett was born.

SOMETIMES YOU FALL, SOMETIMES YOU NEED TO KNOW WHEN TO GET DOWN

Wesley retells the end of his time with the Patriots with a wry smile now. It was September 5, 2009. It was the day for final cuts. Coach Belichick summoned Wesley to his office. Wesley was pretty sure going in that he was going to be released. He had been signed just to a one-year contract in the spring, so he knew his position on the team was tenuous at best.

"Wesley, the last four years you've done everything we asked you to do. You played fullback, tight end, special teams, everywhere on the offensive line. Shoot, I wish I had 53 guys just like you," Coach Belichick said after Wesley sat down.

"Coach, you've got one guy just like me sitting right here. And I'm pretty sure you're about to fire me," Wesley quipped.

"You're not going to make this easy on me, are you, Wes?" Coach Belichick shot back.

They proceeded to have a nice conversation. "But he still fired me," Wesley adds with a chuckle.

Looking back, he also says it was almost a relief when his time with the Patriots ended. He had been in a constant battle to keep a job for four years. He knew it would not last forever. Now, with that battle over, he could turn his full focus to our family—we had Bennett and Ridgeway was on the way—and starting the next phase of his professional life.

He decided to head back to school to get his MBA. When he

was at orientation on campus, he actually got a call that tested him. The Colts wanted to sign him. They wanted him on a plane to Indianapolis.

Wesley prayed about it. We discussed it. I encouraged him to do it—after all, who else could say they blocked for both Tom Brady and Peyton Manning? He was also grappling with how not playing football would affect his self-identity and worth. Ever since he was a child, football was what he was known for. He was used to being a star athlete and succeeding athletically. For the first time, he had run into a brick wall of failure. And he had done so in a very public fashion—something that most of us don't have to contend with in our personal failures.

"No one understands," I remember Wesley saying at the time. "If a guy loses his job at the bank or as a salesman, they don't see their name scrolling on the bottom of ESPN stressing for all of the world to read that he just got fired."

Wesley prayed about it some more. I prayed for God to guide him. In the end, he was ready to move on. He turned down the Colts, and our next chapter began. While earning his MBA, Wesley took on a fellowship with one of his life mentors, Coach Mal Moore. It was an adjustment, but Wesley knew deep inside that he was much more than a football player—and he wanted to prove it to the world.

He also understood it was his time to hang up his cleats—to get off the top of the pyramid, so to speak. There are seasons in life, and it's important we don't try to overextend ours. But it's also critical to recognize when stepping away from something—or yielding an opportunity to someone who is better suited for it—is the right thing to do.

This was a lesson I learned cheerleading in high school. My senior year, I was coming off of my first honors as national cheerleader and world cheerleader of the year, respectively. At my high school, positional opportunities within the cheer squad had been based on seniority up to that point—that is, seniors literally got the coveted spot on top of the pyramid. As a senior and as captain, it was my turn.

However, I didn't think that was how things should work. While I was the captain, we were a team. And each member of the team should do what was best for our collective success. No one needed to wait their turn—and no one was entitled to an opportunity based on something like seniority rather than merit.

There was a girl who was a better fit to top the pyramid based on her skillset. She would be better in that position for the squad's competitiveness. So, I removed myself and gave her the assignment. I put the best person in the best position for the team to win.

Throughout life, we need to be willing to put aside hollow things like convention, ego, and hubris to be a change agent. When someone else is better for a role and will do better in a role, change agents step aside. Title holders dig in, because they don't want to lose the title—whether they're well-suited for that title or not.

Remember the words of 1 Peter 4:10.

Each of you has been blessed with one of God's many wonderful gifts to be used in the service of others. Use your gift well.

God calls us to use the unique gifts He has granted us to do good—to be of service to other people, who are all made in God's image. Change agents do just that. Title holders let their gifts waste away, while impeding opportunities for others to use their gifts.

Another verse speaks to this lesson.

My friends, you were chosen to be free. So, don't use your freedom as an excuse to do anything you want. Use it as an opportunity to serve one another in love.—Galatians 5:13.

Take Nathan, for example. Talk about someone with a servant's heart. Wesley met Nathan—a walk-on player for the Tide—his freshman year of college at the team's summer camp. They had most of the same classes together, being only a handful of student-athletes in the College of Business school, and their study halls and labs usually coincided. Wesley says it did not take him long to figure out that Nathan was not only the smartest person he had ever met but also the most loyal friend. He would drop whatever he was doing to help you, no matter the personal expense to himself.

As a walk-on, he might not have gotten as much playing time on the field, but Nathan was a key part of the football team's locker room as a leader and helped hold everyone together while on campus. However, that's not the biggest thing that made him a change agent.

In 2004, Nathan decided to forgo his final year of football eligibility to enlist in the military. Wesley will never forget Nathan telling him that he was going to join the Marines and fight for our country. Following 9/11, he wanted to serve—no matter the personal sacrifice. Nathan went on to become a Rifle Platoon Commander and during his deployment in Iraq was awarded the Navy Commendation Medal with combat "V" for Valor as a First Lieutenant in recognition of his actions while in combat.

Freedom is a gift—one that we can never take for granted. We have an overriding obligation to use our freedom wisely and responsibly. This entails us remembering our "why." We must relentlessly pursue purpose, not empty pleasure.

Let's look back at Wesley's career at Alabama as an example. At several stops along the way, he could have jumped ship in order to advance his own short-term interests.

He went into his freshman year thinking he was going to be a starter. He ended up not playing a snap.

The team was, on the surface at least, poised to compete for the National Championship. They ended with a losing record and not coming close to even being bowl eligible that season. In half of the seasons he played, the team was barred from postseason competitions entirely. And the team's recruiting competitiveness was hamstrung by scholarship sanctions.

Additionally, one of the big selling points of Alabama had always been coaching stability. Coach Spurrier at Florida was rumored to be thinking about an NFL exit when Wesley was making his decision—which turned out to be true the following year, but Alabama seemingly did not have the same risk of a coaching carousel. In the end, Coach DuBose was fired after Wesley's first season, and he would go on to have four coaches in a historically turbulent firestorm for the storied program.

Wesley had every reason in the world to transfer to a school where he could have found what he initially signed up for. Stability. Winning. The best possible spotlight to elevate his path to the NFL.

But his commitment was to Alabama. And that was not changed by any of the circumstances outside his control. His mission remained. He had a duty to fulfill his responsibility to the team with passion and integrity. He signed up for a job, and there was no world in which he was not going to finish that job and keep his commitment.

That's what I think of when I visit the University of Alabama's campus now and see Wesley's handprints and footprints by Denny Chimes. Every permanent team captain in program history has their prints preserved in stone there. Some of them have national championship rings or other hardware to their names. But seeing Wesley's name there fills me with pride knowing the leadership he provided to the program in some of its toughest years.

He could have chosen the easy road. But he believed in the university. He believed in the program. And he believed that his commitment meant something larger than football.

Character and strength truly shine through in choppy waters, not during calm seas. Real leaders, *change agents*, push through when things are tough.

Wesley knew being a team captain was much more than a title. It was a promise to his teammates, the program, and the fanbase. He kept that promise at every turn. He was a force for good in the role. He assumed responsibility, owned the space, and saw the job through. That's what a leader does—even when you know you won't reap the benefits of your own leadership.

In Wesley's case, the program stabilized—and then Coach Moore brought that same "Nicholas Saban" to Tuscaloosa two years after Wesley left campus. Since then, Coach Saban has won six national championships with the Crimson Tide—and we're still counting.

Knowing your "why" and ensuring your actions lead back to it is a hard thing. But it always pays off in the end.

CHAPTER 6

Control What You Can Control

ONE OF THE HARDEST THINGS is accepting the fact that there are things in life that are out of our control. We should focus on controlling what we can control—not trying to control what we can't. But that is easier said than done.

Things happen *around* us every day. Things happen *to* us every day. Things happen that we don't even realize happened. And we only have control over a limited amount of our life.

Yes, this can be frustrating. Yes, this can be scary. For some, this can even be unthinkable. However, it's a reality for each and every one of us, whether we like it or not.

Interestingly, we have a tendency to place more weight on the things we cannot control, obsessing over them or using them to predetermine our own inability to succeed. If we actually focus on and take responsibility for the things we can and should control, then we will actually have to put in the work. Ultimately, is our fear that if we begin to move the needle—sometimes ever so slowly—to achieve a desired result but are then unsuccessful, that we will have no one to blame but ourselves? To avoid accountability, we make excuses and point to things we can do absolutely nothing about.

By focusing on things outside of our control (in addition to giving us an excuse not to put in the work), we give up our own ability to protect our peace. We allow these things to be a constant disruptor, making us feel uneasy and inadequate in our own heads.

Unfortunately, we are all guilty of this more times than we would like to admit. I certainly find myself falling back into the same trap at times, despite my best efforts. I am sure you have heard the tried-and-true Serenity Prayer before, but it really is important to focus on these words.

God, grant me the serenity to accept the things I cannot change, the courage to change the things I can, and the wisdom to know the difference.

A key to living our purpose can be found in facing the truth of our finite control and then being empowered—rather than feeling helpless—by the newfound perspective that results from it. Once we acknowledge that there are things we cannot change and understand what we actually can change, life becomes more straightforward. We can focus on the things that are under our control, maximizing our outcomes.

However, we always have to be vigilant about not letting ourselves get distracted.

Think about it this way—your life is a series of choices that you are in control of making, in addition to events outside your control that are not your responsibility. So, don't be burdened by them. Give those to God. Let that realization lift weight off of your shoulders.

Sometimes what seem to be the smallest things can make the biggest difference.

Near the end of my junior year in high school, I was offered the chance to go to Australia. A Christian school from Montgomery was traveling there to play football, and they wanted to bring some cheerleaders from Alabama with them to be on the sidelines for and perform at their games. I went to an interest meeting about the trip. There was one hiccup. It would cost each cheerleader $3,000 to participate. And I didn't have $3,000.

My parents worked tirelessly to provide for my sisters and me, and they made sure we had what we needed. But with four girls, all of whom participated in some kind of extracurricular activity, $3,000 was a lot of money. If I was going to participate, I wanted to be able to pay for it myself—or at least help pay for most of it. I thought about asking to borrow some money from my grandparents. And I even began to formulate a plan to make some extra money through a side hustle selling snacks at school.

Before I could take the next step, God intervened.

I was driving back from school, listening to a local FM radio station based in Enterprise, WKMX.

They said they were having a contest. The prize was $3,000 exactly. The winner just had to call in and be a certain number caller.

All I was in control of in the grand scheme of things was whether I called in or not. I was pretty sure God was sending me a sign. And I also knew that calling in couldn't hurt—the worst that could happen was I still needed $3,000. I had already bought some candy in bulk and was planning on selling it at school to get my start on the amount I needed.

I called in right when I got home. I was the correct number caller. I won $3,000, the same amount I needed to pay for the trip to Australia.

There was a lot out of my control in this situation. How many others would call into the show. How quickly people would call in. But I didn't fixate on any of that. I focused on executing my part—calling in. Boy was that a simple task. But it wasn't automatic by any stretch of the imagination. It would have been easy to calculate the chances of winning and simply not try. I called despite the things out of my control. And it worked out. The odds would've said that it was likely to go the other way.

Think about how many times in life we don't pick up the phone, because we believe that our ability to achieve success is slim. That trip was not only a once-in-a-lifetime experience, but Grandmomma, my maternal grandmother, was able to use what money she would have likely allowed me to borrow for herself to go as our chaperone. We had the absolute best time. She went to be with the Lord much too soon in her life. And it wasn't until later that I really realized that there was a ripple effect of me picking up the phone that day that I would have never imagined. Time with my grandmother that I will *forever* cherish.

God's got a plan. And in life, we're called to pick up the phone.

This is a critical component of faith. Trusting that God's plan is the best plan. Always. So, even when things are out of our personal control or don't go exactly how we would have scripted them, we must trust and rejoice in Him, while staying focused on doing our part. Find the things you can change, the things you can do something about, the things that go to the heart of who you actually are. Doing our part is sometimes small and sometimes big. And staying focused on that is easier preached than practiced.

But you'd be amazed by what's possible when we follow God's plan and everything else works itself out. This returns us to the topic of being our best. That's the "what" in what we are responsible for.

But how do we be our best?

This is a lesson PaPa, my paternal grandfather, taught me when I was growing up.

It really began from an early age with my weekly routine. Every Sunday before church, I would go over to MaMa and PaPa's house. MaMa would make oatmeal. It was my favorite. She would add in blueberries we picked from bushes in her garden (the garden also had corn, okra, peas, butterbeans, tomatoes, and potatoes). Then came some raisins and a dusting of brown sugar to top it off. To this day, no oatmeal has ever tasted as good to me as MaMa's. I still get oatmeal every time I am traveling and see it in a breakfast buffet, because I know it will immediately trigger those Sunday morning memories and make it feel like home.

Being at MaMa and PaPa's house brought with it reminders of the time in which they grew up—during the Great Depression. They internalized those dire economic times and the need to do more with less. This manifested itself in several noticeable ways. MaMa to this day always washes off tinfoil and reuses it, for example. I remember as a child hanging up aluminum foil on a line for her so it would dry and be ready for another round of use. She would also pour milk into scrambled eggs to make them go further. And PaPa was regimented about everything around the house. "Y'all, don't use too many squares of toilet paper" was a common refrain to hear for my sisters and me. He would even take already-little pieces of chocolate and use his pocketknife to cut them into slivers for all of his grandchildren to split—and he had *a lot* of grandchildren.

Those Sunday mornings were crucial parts of my development, including my journey to accepting Jesus as my Lord and Savior. From just about the time I could read, PaPa would help me study the Bible verse I was supposed to memorize for Sunday School or learn the answers I was supposed to recite for my Catechism while MaMa cooked. He and I would sit in their old-school den, a small room right off the kitchen. It had wooden bookcases on one side and was the only room in their house with a television. I took learning the Catechism very seriously. I would even study during the week just to make sure I was prepared for Sunday morning. The hard work and diligence paid off. At age seven, I became the youngest ever member of our church to complete Catechism class.

That little den was also where PaPa would flip through Norman Rockwell books with my sisters and me. He'd pick out an illustration and task us with telling a story about what we thought was happening in the picture. There was also a book of classic nursery rhymes and stories, which we would read together. My sister, Norma, will have that book at her house one day. She outsmarted the rest of us by placing a sticky note in the book stating that she would give it a loving home once MaMa and PaPa were done loving it—and then she got PaPa to sign it. Well played, Norma. Well played.

There were a lot of memories made at MaMa and PaPa's house. There were a lot of lessons learned there, too. However, it's one specific talk with PaPa that has stuck with me the most throughout life's peaks and valleys.

THE GIRLS STATE FAMILY

I was selected as one of Enterprise High School's two delegates to Alabama Girls State the spring of my junior year. Our school's librarian carried out the selection process, which included an essay and then interviews. Each school has a different selection process, some more competitive than others. But every school gets the same number of delegates.

The Girls State program is an incredible nationwide initiative run by the American Legion Auxiliary. Girls State develops leadership and patriotism in young women across America while educating them about our system of government, instilling a greater understanding of American traditions, and fostering civic pride. The selfless women who volunteer their time each summer to give delegates this life-changing opportunity are literally like family. And when you become a delegate, you not only leave with an incredible experience, but you leave as part of the Girls State family too.

The first ever Girls State was conducted in 1938, while Alabama began participating in 1942. The state's inaugural programming was held at Camp Grandview Park with less than 70 girls in attendance. When I attend annually now as an alumna speaker, there are more than 350 girls in attendance at Troy University.

However, it was 1946 that brought Alabama Girls State to Montgomery's Huntingdon College for the first time. The program was still held there annually in 1999 when I attended as a delegate.

I can vividly recall pulling into Huntingdon's parking lot that summer heading into my senior year of high school. I was nervous, intimidated, and terrified.

I was coming straight to Girls State following that cheerleading trip to Australia—the one that I was able to attend because I happened to "pick up the phone." I was barely going to make it during the slotted check-in time frame so there was no time for me to spend at home in Enterprise to pack my clothes or prepare for the weeklong programming. My mom had loaded just about every piece of clothing I owned into our old tank of a Suburban. I had actually backed it into my Firebird the previous summer taking a carload of girls to a dance camp in Ozark. I literally totaled the side of my trusty Firebird, but there was barely a scratch on the Suburban. It was a two-toned color—a silverish light grey on top, with a darker grey on the bottom. A red pinstripe separated the two hues. The back of the Suburban had two doors. They swung open, and my clothes were nearly falling out.

Right there in the college's parking lot by its newest dorm, I laid out my suitcase on the asphalt and began to pick and choose clothes from the trunk that would be staying with me at Girls State for the coming days. It was a mortifying experience. I felt like everyone on campus was staring at me as I waded through the back of the Suburban, searching for outfits that would help put my best foot forward. I certainly wasn't off to the best start, at least in my mind.

Other girls had already made and began displaying their campaign materials. Signs adorned the grassy areas on both sides of the sidewalk winding up to the dorm entrance. Sheets emblazoned with painted campaign messages billowed from windows. And all I had were some blank posterboards and markers. Another cornerstone of Girls State is that each delegate writes and presents her own bill, and I had just drafted mine during the car ride to Montgomery. I still did not have a speech written about my bill. I was behind the curve, and the feelings of discomfort and inadequacy began to swell up.

I made the long walk to what would be my dorm room for the week. On the sidewalk outside, girls were chalking in support of their own candidacies—seemingly for every office known to man, plus some I'm pretty sure no one had ever heard of. Some girls were even standing outside holding signage and asking other delegates for their votes. I made it inside and trekked down the hall, past girls from all over the state. Girls that, in my perspective at that very second, were better prepared than me and better positioned to succeed. I assumed that meant they were *better* than me. I felt inadequate. I momentarily lost focus of being my best. My ears were ringing. My heart was pounding. My eyes blurred as I saw girls' campaign posters lining the walls.

As I got to my room, I met my roommate, who was really nice, and began to settle in—and settle down. I sat down on my bed, took a deep breath, and closed my eyes to the world. That's when I remembered what PaPa had taught me.

I was transported from that moment to a couple of weeks earlier. In preparation for Girls State, I met with a few mentors about current events and political subjects that might come up during the program. We discussed issues about which I would need to be knowledgeable, and I asked questions about different perspectives and belief systems.

I met with my Uncle Mike at his office. And I met with my dad in his study.

Finally, I called PaPa and told him that I wanted to discuss Girls State with him. I explained the program to him and previewed some of the topics on which I wanted to touch. He told me to come over after church on Sunday, so we could spend a few hours talking about issues.

This was a more formal conversation than our pre-church visits in his den, so we sat in the living room after MaMa made us sandwiches.

The 2000 presidential election cycle was starting to gear up by then, so some of what we discussed was driven by candidates and would-be candidates of that time. On the Republican side, that contest wound up featuring George W. Bush, John McCain, Alan Keyes, Steve Forbes, Lamar Alexander, Orrin Hatch, Dan Quayle, John Kasich, Elizabeth Dole, Gary Bauer, Herman Cain, and Bob Smith, before quickly winnowing to an effectively two-person race. On the other side of the aisle, Al Gore—the sitting Vice President at the time—had a much easier path to the nomination, really only facing one primary challenger.

Looking back, 1999 was an eventful year across the board in the United States, both inside and outside the world of politics. When I was preparing to head to Girls State that May, Bill Clinton had just been impeached by the House and then acquitted by the Senate months earlier. President Clinton was then cited for contempt of court in a civil trial. The horror of Columbine occurred in April. And the United States, alongside NATO partners, was at war in Kosovo.

When PaPa and I finished our discussion, I began packing up my notebook. Almost offhandedly, he asked me, "Are you going to run for something?"

I hesitated. "I don't think so."

"Why not?"

"Well, I want to, but..."

I started listing reasons why I was intimidated. I ticked through the challenges involved in running. This girl's parents have a fancy job. Another girl goes to that prestigious school. That girl lives in an exclusive neighborhood. Or the girls whose résumés boasted titles I never held.

My grandfather stopped me as I began to chatter on about why I thought that I would be overmatched.

"None of that matters. It doesn't matter how much money is in your parents' bank account, what zip code you live in, or where you go to school. There are four things that matter in life and that will ultimately determine your path: your character; your integrity; your work ethic; and the way you treat people. Young lady, I have good news for you. You, and only you, are in control of all four of those things."

That lesson might be the single most important one I've ever learned. And it's a lesson that God calls each of us to follow.

There is no doubt there is an endless number of things out of our control in life. That can be intimidating and overwhelming until you remember that the things that do matter in life are in your control. The things that actually define who you are as a person, a friend, a mentor, and a believer are absolutely, 100% up to YOU. So, focus on those things—the ones that you can control. This will help you feel your best and help you be your best.

That's exactly what I did in my dorm room at Girls State that first day. I collected myself, remembered what PaPa told me, and, after some internal back-and-forth, ultimately, I decided to run for governor.

Girls State sees every delegate assigned to a home city and one of two fictitious political parties. Each party then holds primary election contests for a range of positions, from local offices such as mayor to statewide positions. Campaigning, especially back then before social media, consisted of true grassroots, retail politicking. Making individual overtures to fellow delegates, making a personal connection, really listening to them, and forming an authentic relationship was key. I worked tirelessly, keeping what PaPa told me at the front of my mind.

Then, there came the speeches. And what we called "whistle stops," which were essentially lightning rounds of questions from other delegates. And more speeches. I never had any formal public speaking or debate training. The only time I had really addressed a crowd while on stage previously was through my experience as Little Miss National Peanut. I guess it paid off in the end. I won my party's nomination for governor.

The general election at Girls State was a game of strategy. Each party had an even number of delegates. So, the most straightforward path to victory was holding onto your own party delegates' votes, while trying to swing a few members of the opposition party to vote your way. That's where authentic relationship building throughout the week really came in handy. If you had not put in the work early in the program, it would be too late in the final stage to try and truly connect with people.

The general election culminated in a debate between the gubernatorial nominee of the other party and me. She was highly qualified and had impressive experience in Youth Legislature. I thought she had a higher pedigree than me.

I again ran PaPa's lesson through my head. I had to keep repeating those words internally to keep the feelings of inadequacy at bay. Another wave of intimidation subsided.

That was a lightbulb moment. All I could control—and the key to succeeding—came down to being me. It was all about leaning into the strengths God did give me, not focusing on the ones I was without. I worked diligently to be the best version of myself, and that is when it finally started to click. By doing just that—working to be the best version of myself—I was actually following God's plan.

I can't really remember what topics were discussed during the debate or what our dialogue consisted of. But, at the end of the day, the votes were tallied—and I was elected governor of Alabama Girls State in 1999.

That achievement did not just happen in the moment, however. Success occurs when preparation meets opportunity. My weeks of reading up on current events and political issues—and discussing them with mentors to gain different perspectives and deeper understanding—had prepared me more than I realized heading into the program.

From there, I handled what I could control. I focused on living out my character. I acted with integrity. I worked as hard as I could. And I treated people with respect. And everything else fell into place. I know that if I had chosen to spend my time focused on other things, it could have easily gone a different way.

Fast forward 24 years, and my Girls State lessons, experience, memories, and friendships have lasted to this day.

You and only you control your attitude. You and only you control if you are worthy of someone's trust. You and only you control whether you keep your word. You and only you control how hard you work. You and only you control whether you show people kindness. You and only you control...well, most of the things that matter. Think about that for a minute. Not someone else. Just *you*.

I am not saying that there aren't situations or events that make these things really hard. There absolutely are. But after a certain age, no one is responsible for how you handle them but you.

In committee hearings in the Senate, I have found myself telling witnesses that I want them to "own their space." That means I want to hear them take responsibility for their role in whatever we are discussing. Don't tell me what someone else did wrong or should have done differently, tell me what you could have or should have done differently. One of the hard things you are called to do is *own your space.*

In life, it is rare that the ultimate objective of a course of actions is as clearly defined as being elected as governor of Girls State. Most of the time, we also reap the rewards—or bear the consequences—of our actions on a longer timeline. In our day-to-day routines, we act out of habit. What we do becomes second nature. And the overarching results of what we do can be out of immediate sight—and, thus, out of mind.

This reality is why it is imperative to be disciplined when there is seemingly nothing on the line. Be disciplined even when you don't think it matters. Be relentlessly focused on controlling what you can control. If you let the things in your control slip, there will be repercussions—whether you suffer them in the short run or down the road.

One of my favorite Bible verses is 2 Timothy 1:7.

For God did not give us a spirit of timidity, but a spirit of power, of love, and of self-discipline.

The best way to stay disciplined is to create a process, set a standard, and be consistent in executing. If your norm is your best, that becomes the rule.

There is no doubt that I am not going to get it right every day, but I can promise you that it will not be for a lack of trying.

Remember, perfect is not possible. So, prioritize process over outcome. This will make mistakes the exception—not the expectation. And it will make success the inevitability—not the improbability.

Think about it this way—if consistency was a place, it would have very few residents.

How do you become a member of this exclusive community?

Pay attention to the little things. Consistency—and greatness—is achieved by piecing together a lot of things that individually might seem small but that matter a great deal collectively. They form a pattern and something larger than their individual sums when they are combined the right way. Consider how expert quiltmakers—like the ladies of Gee's Bend in Wilcox County, Alabama—take strips and scraps of assorted cloth and fabric and manage to turn them into masterpieces when woven together. In this way, details are a lost art.

I learned this lesson from an early age through dance.

CHAPTER 7

Don't Dance Around the Details

I STARTED DANCING AT 18 MONTHS OLD. It's really only recently that it struck me how young I was when I began dancing. But when your mom owns the dance studio and has to be at work, so do you. So, I was literally surrounded by the world of dance from before I can even remember. I never really had a choice to begin with. But I loved it from the start.

Many people have a similar activity that is synonymous with their childhood. It might be a sport, or for some, it was showing cattle, participating in choir, or taking piano lessons. For me, it was always dance.

We know that the vast majority of us won't perform or play professionally, but we do these things anyway. That's because of the lifelong lessons we learn and memories we make along the way.

These types of extracurricular activities take up a great deal of time and energy during our formative years. And they help us all grow and become who we are as adults. We remember the late-night games and practices, especially when we had a big test the next day at school. We recall the nerves before taking the stage, field, court, or mat. The feeling of agony when we didn't do our best. The disappointment when they call someone else's name. Then there were big trips we'll never forget to tournaments or competitions—those were our vacations really. At least they were for me. In between the memories, during the smallest and most mundane of moments, we learned, we grew, and we were slowly shaped by our activities and experiences.

Dance taught me dedication, discipline, how to take criticism, and what it takes to improve, including welcoming feedback early and often, not quitting when things get hard, and—probably most importantly—having a good attitude.

Mom's dance studio was like a second home for me. Before I was born, she was a dance teacher there when it was under previous ownership. One day, she bought the studio in tandem with Ms. Jenny—her mentor, friend, and a fellow dance teacher. They renamed the studio to reflect their newfound business partnership—it became the Jen-Deb School of Dance.

Mom had a passion for her work. She only took a week or so off from teaching dance after I was born. When she returned to the studio, she took me with her. I laid in a playpen in the back of her studio room as she taught her classes. Mom taught all kinds of classes, from tap and ballet to jazz and clogging to creative movement for the younger kids.

The day before I turned eight months old, I took my first steps and was off to the races. By my first birthday, Mom says I was "talking up a storm." I was small—just about 18 pounds at the time. But I moved around quickly, and I was even beginning to imitate the dance classes I was watching from the back of the room.

I was soon enrolled in my first dance class at the studio at just 18 months old.

It was a small cinder block building that backed up to an old movie theater. The studio was split into two classrooms. When you entered the door, there was a small reception area, with a bulletin board featuring newspaper clippings telling the tales of the studio's previous competitions and accolades. You could not miss the old-school TV sitting on a bookcase against the wall. To the right of the entrance, there was a bathroom and an office space. Parents could look into the classrooms through one-way mirrors and watch class from wooden benches that lined the walls in the reception area and a long hallway that spanned the left side of the building. Mom's classroom was closest to the entrance. Ms. Jenny's room was farthest from the entrance and was a tad bit larger.

Even before I was old enough to participate in dance competitions, the studio was where I found myself on Saturdays. If I wasn't practicing, I was put to work in other ways. Running a family-owned small business meant you do just about every odd job that needs doing. So, from an early age, there I was helping Mom do inventory. When I got into elementary school, I began to do more and more. Soon, I cleaned the bathroom, both tiny stalls and toilets included. I tidied up and organized the storage closet that was sandwiched between the classrooms. I swept and mopped the floors. I scrubbed the mats. I did whatever needed to be done. I worked hard, and I quickly learned not to complain about doing so.

I also remember stocking the stash of drinks and snacks in the office. Students and parents could come up to a little service window facing the reception area and get a Coke along with some candy or chips. This was back in the days when a soda cost 50 cents, as did each snack. A single dollar got you a drink and food. We probably should have been drinking water instead, but that's beside the point. The office also stored some extra ballet shoes. When cleaning up the studio after hours and on weekends, I would find ballet shoes strewn about in every nook and cranny imaginable.

Until high school, dance monopolized my time outside of class, besides the time I would spend helping out at Dad's store. When school ended, it was a mad dash to the car, where Mom was waiting to take us directly to the studio. Classes began at 3:30.

I wasn't just taking classes. Sometime later into elementary school, I began to apprentice-teach classes. This largely entailed me shadowing younger dance teachers—high school girls who taught some classes for Mom and Ms. Jenny. I would give them an extra set of hands and help out around their classes. My favorite was helping out with the kindergarten jazz class, which was also the first I ever taught by myself. They were all so adorable. And it made me feel old being one of their teachers.

I would attend dance class myself Monday through Thursday each week after school. Friday afternoons of competition weekends normally entailed traveling. That evening would usually include taking a class at the destination. And we would generally compete all day Saturday. Sometimes the routine brought auditions or more classes. At times, I would have to miss a little school to juggle the travel demands. That just meant making up the schoolwork on top of the already busy schedule. It was grueling. But I loved it.

Especially coming from small-town, rural Alabama, dance was also a unique opportunity for me to see parts of the country I otherwise would not have gotten the opportunity to visit as a child. To me, Dothan was the big city. So, dance opened my eyes to the world beyond the Wiregrass. I had the chance to take classes in Los Angeles. I remember going to Atlanta, Orlando, and Boston for the first time. I competed against the Abby Lee Dance Company. I even traveled internationally to head to a dance competition in Canada and saw the wonder of Niagara Falls.

Probably the most fun I had traveling for dance was in New York. Mom typically took students there each summer, so I had the opportunity to go on several occasions. The first time, I was five years old. On that occasion, I sat in the back of classes and watched as some of Mom's older students learned from local instructors. Soon, I was the one taking classes.

I still have memories of my first Broadway play—it was *Cats*. One year, I saw *The Will Rogers Follies*. I admit that I fell asleep in that one. I felt bad that my parents saved up for me to see it. *Phantom of the Opera* was a different story on a later trip. I wanted to go so badly, but tickets were in especially high demand. We ended up only being able to find two tickets, and Mom and Ms. Jenny gave them to Holly—Ms. Jenny's oldest daughter—and me. I felt so grown up attending a Broadway play with just that teenage girl who I looked up to.

We did all of the touristy things in New York. The Statue of Liberty. The Empire State Building. And our competitions were typically held at the Marriott Marquis in Times Square. Even visiting as an adult years later, just seeing those escalators brought the nostalgia flooding back.

Those were also very different times. We saw the World Trade Center. It still feels surreal going back to the city now, knowing Bennett and Ridgeway will experience New York—and the world—so differently than we did in the previous century.

In those days, parents could walk their child right up to the gate at the airport and then send you unescorted on your way to a destination. That's how I visited Michigan for the first time.

Dance also introduced me to friends who felt like family. My teammates came from all over the Wiregrass. They were from Enterprise, Elba, Samson, and Geneva. And the competition circuit connected me with girls from across Alabama. This goes to show you that life does indeed come full circle, because as I traveled the state on the campaign trail more than 20 years later, I reconnected with several people I remembered competing with and against.

The fond, lifelong memories aside, dance taught me invaluable lessons and formed building blocks on which I still strive to grow and improve.

I love dance because of the technical and emotional aspects of it. To achieve mastery—and to turn your craft into an artform on stage—you had to be equally disciplined in both facets.

You learned to express yourself in an intentional manner, while being mentally sharp and regimented in your physical technique. I also came to relish the opportunity to conquer my fears that dance presented. As I would stand off-stage, seconds away from performing, I could both hear and feel my heart about to leap out of my chest. I learned to love it. Pushing through the nerves and harnessing the adrenaline became part of the thrill.

It also allowed me to be a part of something larger than myself. There are few things more beautiful than a well-choreographed, well-executed dance coming together on stage.

I inherently learned to control what I could control through dance. I was not the most naturally flexible. I practiced my technique ceaselessly. I stretched and trained to improve myself, constantly pushing my limits further. And I was taught to welcome constructive feedback and be eager to make corrections and improvements.

What seemingly were the tiniest details in dance mattered the most. How pointed your toes were. Being on the perfectly exact count. Moving in precisely the choreographed way. Being meticulous with how high you kick. Knowing when your role in the team was to stand out or not be noticed.

There was always a larger vision in dance, and it was fulfilled by paying attention to the small details.

THE LITTLE THINGS PAVE THE WAY TO THE BIG LEAGUES

To be detail-oriented requires discipline. Wesley's experience playing for the Patriots under Coach Bill Belichick gave us a front-row seat to why this is so important.

The first thing that Wesley explains to people about Coach Belichick is that there is no one who works harder or puts in more time to be his best and excel at his profession than him. Even during the offseason, anyone driving by the Patriots' practice facility in Foxboro will likely see Coach Belichick's vehicle in the parking lot, often by itself, late into the night. Coach Belichick drove a purple RAV4 the entire time Wesley was a Patriot. Coach would be there still past 10:00 pm, putting in the extra work that provides a championship edge. He studied film constantly, breaking down practice and game tapes to the most microscopic detail.

That time in the film room also helps Coach Belichick analyze things in real time that most would not be able to pick up on.

After practice one day, Coach Belichick walked up to Wesley.

"Today, when we were running a 34-lead zone, you were taking a 12-inch lead step," Coach told Wesley flatly. "Now, you know that running play calls for a six-inch lead step. If you don't fix that tomorrow, you won't have a job."

He had noticed a six-inch difference in a single step. And he knew even that seemingly minute factor could be the difference between a successful play or a complete bust.

Wesley also appreciated the directness with which Coach Belichick communicated. You never had to guess where you stood with him. The brutally honest approach he took with players fostered accountability around the team—and allowed players to receive constructive feedback in a no-nonsense manner that lends itself to clear-cut improvements being made.

"There was no passive-aggressiveness there," Wesley adds. "No guesswork. You knew exactly what he expected out of you. He would teach you the best technique and give you the best tools to do your job. And he would tell you precisely what your job was. Six inches. I can fix that. That's 100% in my control. I was grateful to get that kind of candor on and off of the field from Coach Belichick. Most coaches—even if they picked up on that detail—would avoid the confrontation and just cut you. But that doesn't help you or the team get better."

The next thing Wesley will tell you about Coach Belichick is that he does very much care for his players. He is laser-focused on the things under his control that he believes will affect winning football games. That's why he has never enjoyed dealing with the media—he doesn't view it as something that can help the team achieve its goals. And he doesn't really try to hide his feelings on the subject.

However, the gruff persona you might see on television in

exchanges with the press doesn't properly capture who Coach Belichick is behind his trademark sweatshirt.

I still remember him calling us right after the tornado on April 27, 2011. Wesley had no longer been a Patriot for about 18 months at that point. But there was Coach Belichick on the phone, asking Wesley about Bennett, Ridgeway, and me. Interactions like that helped us face recovery more than people could ever imagine.

And that call was after Coach Belichick wrote Wesley a letter of recommendation for his MBA program application. Fresh off of cutting Wesley from the Patriots, Coach did not owe him anything. However, he knew what Wesley was capable of.

Character. Integrity. Work ethic. And the way you treat people.

The results speak for themselves. Coach Belichick has the most Super Bowl wins as a head coach in NFL history at six, plus two rings as defensive coordinator for the New York Giants in the 1980s under Coach Bill Parcells. Coach Belichick holds the records for the most Super Bowl appearances and playoff wins as a head coach in league history. He is a future member of the Pro Football Hall of Fame in Canton, Ohio. And he has accomplished all of these accolades with the Patriots while being the organization's de facto general manager in addition to his coaching duties. This means he has even broader responsibilities—and more is under his control. This is something he embraces and owns rather than running away from it. And it's part of why he has achieved greatness.

How the little things intertwine in your life can make or break you. If every piece is rock solid—if you achieve consistency—you will have an indestructible chain. However, if you have just one weak link, the entire thing can fall apart.

In working to be *your* best at all times, you can become *the* best without even realizing it.

This is why we must sweat the small stuff. It is focusing on and executing the little things that actually allow you to do the big ones.

This is a maxim as old as time.

Consider the message of Luke 16:10.

Whoever can be trusted with very little can also be trusted with much, and whoever is dishonest with very little will also be dishonest with much.

I learned how true this is during my collegiate internship with Senator Shelby's office in Washington.

It was the summer of 2003. I was heading into my senior year of college and had landed the internship after applying for a class credit through the political science department. Girls State first sparked my passion for public service in high school. Then, SGA at the University of Alabama made me realize that it was possible for me to be involved, which got me interested in pursuing other opportunities to expand my horizons in the field.

Now, for those who are unfamiliar with congressional internships—many interns come to the Hill with dreams of writing high-level policy memos, of helping draft groundbreaking legislation, and of engaging in deep philosophical debate with peers. What you quickly realize is that most internships consist of, well, the little things. You get coffee. You bring back the staff's lunch order. You make copies and—back then, at least—help send faxes. You update the Christmas card list. You escort visitors around and give them tours of the complex. And if you prove yourself, you might even get to answer phones at the front desk.

The work isn't glamorous. And it occurs amid a vibrant social scene in DC at a time in collegiate life when most interns have never been left to fend for themselves in that big of a city. The long and short of the situation is that it can seem easy to put yourself on autopilot during the day and get wrapped up in having fun after hours.

Looking back, I can say with certainty that I would not be a US Senator today if I took that easy route during my internship 20 years ago.

Now, I'll admit, I had some fun as an intern. And I cherish the friendships I made at the time that have stood the test of time.

But, I took the work seriously, and I did not waver from controlling what I could control.

On the last day of the internship, Senator Shelby came up to me. This was surprising in and of itself, because he probably hadn't said three words to me the entire internship.

"You," he said.

I looked around. Was he talking to me? No way. Who is behind me?

He was still looking straight at me and continued speaking.

"They say you come early and stay late," Senator Shelby said.

Goodness. He really was talking to me. This was no longer a drill.

"Yes, sir," I managed to respond after the shock wore off just a smidge.

"They say you have a good attitude no matter what they give you," he continued.

I told him that I was happy to help. I thought silently to myself that PaPa taught me well.

"They say you think down the road and around the corner. You have things prepared that they haven't even asked you for yet," the Senator added.

"Thank you, sir."

Then came a silent pause that seemed to last an eternity.

"You...you can come back," he concluded.

Those four words changed my life. He just handed me a job offer that would forever alter what was possible for me. And he did so because I had controlled the things I could control—which at the time seemed to be little, insignificant things. Instead of focusing on what I didn't get to do as an intern, I focused on what I *did* get to do. And doing my best at those little things ultimately made a big difference.

I did not show up to the internship with the mindset of a title holder. I was not there to put it on my résumé, go to Union Pub every afternoon, and move on after those few weeks passed by.

I had worked hard. In fact, I had gone above and beyond. I was not just present more than required—I was diligent during the time I was present, too.

I also showed up with a good attitude. It would have been easy—natural, even—to let what could accurately be categorized as grunt work bring me down. But instead, I took the mindset that no type of work in the office was beneath me.

And finally, I was intentional. I asked myself "why" after being assigned tasks and soon learned to anticipate what would be needed of me in the future.

The little things truly are a big deal.

This lesson extended over the following 12 months. I was SGA president much of that senior year of college. And I tried to be my best in that role, aiming to use the opportunity to leave things better than I found them. I sought to be a change agent rather than a title holder.

Work ethic. Character. Integrity. The way I treat people. Attitude. Intentionality. I focused on piecing all of it together.

After graduating in the spring of 2004, it came time to take Senator Shelby up on his offer. I loaded up my mom's GMC Envoy with all of my possessions and drove directly from Tuscaloosa to Washington, DC.

Understand this, however—I had no idea what job I would be doing in the office. Not a clue. All I knew was that I had a job, and I wanted to serve.

I assumed that I would be sitting at the front desk as a staff assistant. That would have been an honor. It's a great place for young people to start in a congressional office.

I showed up to the office on my first day and waited in the reception area. Senator Shelby's office was in the Hart building at the time, a few floors down from where my office is now.

After a few minutes, it was my time to meet with him. I sat down in his office across from him.

"Katie, you are now my deputy press secretary. Ready to get started?"

Well, I guess it was a good thing I was sitting down.

Ready? I was not a Public Relations major. I had never even stepped foot in the College of Communications. That was my first line of thought.

My second was a flash of fear. I'm going to fail, I thought. I don't know the first thing about this.

I slowed myself down. Well, I do know how to write. I can learn what I don't know. No one will outwork me. I will control what I can control.

Senator Shelby then briefly explained how he came to his decision, which really got my confidence moving in the right direction.

He received news clips every morning from his staff, and those news clips included mentions of what was happening in his hometown at his alma mater—the University of Alabama. So, he would often see snippets from *The Crimson White*, the student newspaper, about what was happening on campus with SGA or the hot-button issue of the day.

"I've seen you navigate challenging, highly scrutinizing waters with the campus press. If you can duplicate that up here, you'll be just fine," he told me.

From student government spats to the halls of the United States Senate—if you pay attention to the small things, the big things will come. My journey is proof positive. I first walked into a Senate office building as an unpaid intern. And now my name is on the door.

Never lose sight of what we're told in Psalm 16:8:

I keep my eyes always on the Lord. With him at my right hand, I will not be shaken.

In the valleys and daily toil of life, it might not seem like big things are right around the bend. However, we are called to stay the course. This is a hard thing. But it is completely in our control—and no one else's.

CHAPTER 8

The Way You Treat People Matters

THE WAY YOU TREAT PEOPLE is not just under your control. It also matters a great deal.

Our words, interactions, actions, and even our inactions affect much more than our own lives—they directly affect the lives of other people, and they have domino effects on the greater community.

At the end of the day, nothing we do occurs in a vacuum. We are not in a silo, nor are we on an island in life. What we do, who we are, and how we act ultimately ripples out into the world that surrounds us, touching and impacting our family, friends, coworkers, and ultimately people we have never met in different shades of positive or negative.

This is one reason why it is so important to consistently be intentional. We are called to control things that impact our own lives. But we also have a greater responsibility to control things that have additional impacts on others. Chief among those things is how we treat people.

Getting this critical aspect of daily life right can be complicated. People and situations are nuanced, and there is no one-size-fits-all recipe for getting each and every human interaction correct.

However, there is one universal maxim that is about as close as it gets to perfect. This adage has stood the test of time, spanning divergent cultures, languages, belief systems, norms, and technological developments.

It was during His Sermon on the Mount that Jesus espoused what we now know as the Golden Rule.

Matthew 7:12 carries His powerful, yet simple, message:

So in everything, do to others what you would have them do to you, for this sums up the Law and the Prophets.

This lesson certainly traveled from a hillside overlooking the Sea of Galilee to the Wiregrass over the course of nearly 2,000 years.

From the earliest age, I was taught the value in having and showing respect and compassion for others. My dad would always remind me that it does not cost you a thing to be kind; however, it can be priceless for the person or people on the receiving end.

The Golden Rule is premised first on self-respect, self-worth, and self-care. If we don't value and treat ourselves correctly, we won't treat others correctly, either.

This is again where you working to be *your* best comes in. Getting this first step right then means you are in position for your best to be reflected outward and shared with others. Your light is ready to shine—and not just for your own benefit.

How you treat others can spread like a contagion for the better or the worse.

If you are channeling your best in interactions, this can be a blessing that spreads several degrees of separation from your direct contact. Just one kernel of kindness can blossom into a radiant garden that brings joy and inspiration to anyone who comes into contact with it.

Likewise, not treating people well can reap repercussions. In life, we can tend to function as sponges. We unconsciously absorb the good and the bad from those around us. So, when we treat someone poorly, we run the extra risk of our negativity being soaked up by that person and passed on to more people down the line.

It can be as simple as the way you start your day or your child's morning. Let's say the family is running behind, someone doesn't have their stuff together for school, or is just moving slower than they should, putting the whole crew on the brink of being late. Tensions escalate and before you know it, there is a shouting match right there in the middle of the kitchen. Frustrations carry into the car ride and continue until that child gets out in the carpool drop-off line. Sound familiar?

You are not only worked up and irritated, but your child has just gotten out of the car with a backpack *and* a morning's worth of baggage that they have no ability to unpack when they walk through that classroom door.

Sure, should they have found their basketball shoes the night before? Without a doubt. But it doesn't change the fact that both your child and you are going to take that negativity with you the majority of the morning—maybe all day. And being on edge may cause an issue between your child and a friend or a teacher. It could cause you to snap at the next person you see. Regardless, it is rare that we can immediately move on from negative things without there being another domino to fall.

This can be a vicious cycle. When someone is rude, do your best to think about what they may be dealing with that day, or in life, that may have led them to behave that way. Then challenge yourself to respond to them in a way that *breaks* that cycle.

When we take a step back and make a conscientious decision to be intentional in reflecting our best in how we treat people, this also means that just one small act of kindness—or grace—can make a world of difference.

The seriousness of these stakes was something that my dad really drove home with me when I was growing up, because it was a lesson that he had to learn the hard way from his father.

It happened around the time my dad was fresh out of college. He started at Livingston University, which is now the University of West Alabama, and then earned his degree at Troy State, known today as Troy University. The family hardware store and boat shop was a small business in every sense of the word, especially back then. There were two full-time employees: my dad plus a mechanic. PaPa floated back-and-forth between there and the family-owned cemetery.

In addition to customers, there were constantly vendors and salespeople coming into the store to try and sell their business products or services. With my dad manning the shop by himself at times, it could become frustrating to have someone else trying to sell to you in your own place of business—while customers and tasks waited.

One day while PaPa was in the store with him, a salesman came in to pitch Dad on some local advertising. His patience had worn thin, and he was fed up that day.

"I was ugly to him. Plain and simple," my dad recounts.

In so many words, Dad told the salesman that he did not have any time to deal with him. He dismissed him without hearing a pitch and without courtesy.

PaPa immediately called my dad into his office, closed the door behind him, and motioned for him to take a seat.

"Julian, I'm really ashamed of you," PaPa told him. "Because that man, whoever he is, is trying to make a living just like you."

That gentleman has a story, too. That gentleman probably has a family he is trying to provide for, PaPa explained in his admonishment.

"It doesn't cost you anything to be nice and courteous to somebody," he continued. "And you never know when that might come back around."

My dad took that lesson to heart. He even tracked the gentleman down to apologize. From then on, Dad always made it a point of personal pride to never be rude to someone like that again. And it's something he taught my sisters and me from an early age. PaPa's one-time message—and the pure disappointment he expressed to my dad—would go on to teach generations.

While we should be kind for selfless reasons alone, treating people well can be gratifying. It can help us feel proud of ourselves and our actions. And it can even be rewarding in external manners, as well. How we treat people is a cornerstone on which our reputation is built, and our reputation is worth more than its weight in gold. Your reputation goes before you and follows behind you, whether you like it or not. Pay attention. And make sure that the ripple effect of the waves you are creating is actually the kind you want. Treating people well can result in tangible benefits in the workplace, in academic settings, and throughout the motley layers of life. Conversely, treating people poorly can cancel out pretty much everything else. You can work hard and achieve mastery of a skill or craft, but it could be all for nothing if you don't practice the Golden Rule.

KINDNESS SHOULD BE BLIND

Kindness in its purest form is never selfish. Strip away self-interest from the equation, and that's when a person's heart of hearts is revealed. How you treat those who you believe cannot benefit you says the most about you.

This is something I have tried to put into practice throughout life, including in my professional career.

After graduating law school in 2013, I joined Johnston Barton Proctor & Rose LLP as an associate. I thought the Birmingham law firm was the right fit for me largely because it was the most family-friendly for a young working mom with two toddlers. I also liked its size, which was about 40 attorneys, and the fact that it had a longstanding reputation in the community—having been in business for more than 85 years. I had found a great mentor in Randy McClanahan, one of the firm's senior partners. Overall, it seemed like the ideal fit for my family and professional needs.

I started at Johnston Barton right after Labor Day. It was my first full-time job as an attorney, and I was eager to settle in, learn, achieve, and impress.

However, only a month or two into practice, the firm's leadership let us know that Johnston Barton would be permanently closing its doors in the coming months.

A torrent of thoughts rushed through my head when they told us.

How would I tell Wesley? How would this impact our kids? I worried for my coworkers, who—like me—would need to find new places to land. I was assured they would help find landing spots for everyone, but I wasn't ready to rest on that.

I was exhausted from the unexpected twists and turns that had already been thrown our way the last few years. The tornado in 2011. In 2012, we moved to Birmingham after Wesley got his MBA and started a new job. I finished law school in spring 2013 after commuting to Tuscaloosa every day for a year, while being Mom to Bennett and Ridgeway each step along the way. At that point, I felt like we had made it through the storm.

But that sense of calm was short-lived. It was moving day yet again.

Almost immediately when we learned the firm would be closing, a type of Hunger Games scramble began. Other law firms began circling to recruit and hire Johnston Barton's employees who were not already committed, and coworkers became competitors in the sprint to secure a job. People grouped up to offer themselves as package deals. Firms would say, "We want you three, but not the fourth." Or, "We can't take you on your own. Who else can you bring with you?"

I was fortunate to already have a mentor at the firm, Randy. He was the kind of boss who wouldn't just tell me when I did something wrong, he would teach me how to do it right. If not for him, many days it felt like I would have been left to essentially fend for myself.

Randy was part of a group that was already in talks to join Butler Snow LLP, an international law firm based in Mississippi. As part of those discussions, Randy worked to ensure my name was part of a group of Johnston Barton attorneys they wanted to bring with them. Including associates in this kind of package deal was typically not an easy sell, because many firms only want to hire attorneys with an existing book of business. Butler Snow, however, was receptive to hiring younger attorneys as part of the group.

God had a plan—and, once again, His plan was the best one.

I got a phone call from an old friend of mine, Sidney.

Flash back to the summer of 2003 with me. It was the first afternoon of my internship with Senator Shelby in Washington, DC. After work, all of the interns in our office went out for dinner—although, that might be a charitable description, because as rising college seniors, the menu of choice seemed to be more of a liquid one.

There we were, socializing and reminiscing on our first hours interning in the US Senate. At some point in our conversation, we started to take notice of the table right behind us.

"They talk just like us," we thought aloud.

Soon, aided in part by the artificial courage resulting from our diet of choice or our natural southern hospitality (which one, we may never know), we turned around and asked them where they were from.

"Mississippi."

That's when I met Sidney. We quickly found out most in their group were interns for Senators Trent Lott and Thad Cochran.

"No way! We're from Alabama."

We became fast friends with the interns from our neighboring state. For the rest of our summer internship period, there wasn't a day that went by when we didn't do something together. I am proud to say our bond lasted past the summer and into life.

More than 10 years later, there was Sidney calling me. He worked at Butler Snow, and leaders at his firm had just informed him and his colleagues they were interested in bringing on attorneys from Johnston Barton. Butler Snow's leadership asked if they knew anyone at the firm in Alabama.

What a small world. Sidney chimed in that he did indeed know someone. "We have to bring her onboard," he said. Sidney became another champion in my hiring to Butler Snow, and before I knew it, I had a new job. Life really does come full circle.

Another lesson to learn from this experience: whether you realize it or not, everyone you meet is a potential reference. It can be your classmate. It can be your teammate's sister. It can be your roommate's brother. It can even be the fellow intern at the table behind you. So, treat people well—no matter who people are.

I took that advice and put it to use at Butler Snow.

I started with the firm in January 2014, along with 17 of my coworkers from Johnston Barton, including Randy. We established a full-service shop for Butler Snow in Birmingham.

One of the things that I loved about Butler Snow from the jump was its collaborative model. The firm is uniquely structured so that coworkers are not competing against one another for clients, unlike the "eat what you kill" game of how most larger firms operate. Everyone has their own lane in which they can best contribute to collective success.

This kind of team-centric atmosphere was put into practice for me quickly. I was appointed to the firm's recruiting committee soon after I arrived, as part of the newcomers being plugged into myriad places where we could make an impact and do our part.

In this role, I was part of the group that would go to law schools to recruit both summer associates and soon-to-be graduates. The recruiting committee was also responsible for conducting interviews in the hiring process.

Now, it's no secret that individuals have every incentive to put their best image forward when interacting with people who they know have the ability to hire them. People interviewing for a job often put on an act. The key for interviewers is to get to the truth—what is this person like when he or she does not believe a job offer is on the line? How would this person behave if hiring authorities were not watching?

You can ask the most cunning questions in an interview to try and elicit grains of truth. You can craft a strategy to get an interviewee to drop their guard a little bit. You might be able to have them partially lift up their mask. But there's still going to be an element of performance, whether artful or not, in the interview room. I've conducted hundreds of interviews in my career, and this is simply human nature.

So, to get a peek behind the curtain, I came up with my own vetting strategy at Butler Snow. Right after an individual finished interviewing with the committee and departed the office, I would go straight to the reception area to speak with the person working the front desk.

I would ask how the interviewee had treated the receptionist both upon arrival and exit. I would ask how the interviewee acted out of earshot and sight of the recruiting committee.

Similarly, I would seek out the gentleman who conducted the logistics and maintenance work for the firm to see if he had any interaction with the interviewee. I would speak to the person who stocked our supplies. And I would even go out to have the same conversation with the security guards in the ground floor lobby.

Many people who put on one heck of a show when they knew a job offer was on the line acted completely differently just seconds before or after when they thought they could not benefit—or lose out—because of how they treated people.

What they displayed in those moments, the moments they felt

free to be themselves, said the most. It was telling if their demeanor changed when they thought someone couldn't help them or—in their eyes—was beneath them.

I remember one instance when this exercise was especially fruitful. It was a young woman who was one of our top recruits—she was someone we wanted to bring onboard, someone we were pitching to just as much as she was interviewing for a job.

Well, until I went to ask how she treated people who she did not think mattered. The story was the same at each stop along the way—she was just downright rude.

She went from a surefire job offer and a likely bidding war for her services to being cut from consideration. All because she failed to practice the Golden Rule. There are unintended consequences—and real value—to just being kind.

This example is also a warning on the pitfalls of being selfish versus selfless in how we approach treating others. The young woman was putting her own interests above others, and that mentality drove how she treated certain people.

Instead, how we treat people should be blind to who is on the receiving end. Every job and every person has value and deserves to be treated as such. Whether you're interacting with your professor or a custodian, your boss or an intern, your mayor or a complete stranger, the kindness and respect with which you treat people should not be determined by their station in life or what you believe they can do for you. I believe it is imperative you treat the man who changes the lightbulb with the same respect you use with the chairman of the firm.

Every person is made in God's image. They matter. And they deserve kindness and respect.

Be intentional about practicing kindness even when you think it can't benefit you, and it'll become second nature for you across the board.

What you might perceive as the smallest act of kindness could make a huge difference for the person on the receiving end. Remember—we never know what someone else is going through in private or in their own head. Sharing your light of compassion and care, even if it is just a passing smile, kind word, or courteous deed, could be the spark someone needs to turn the light on in a dark place. We have the power to uplift others around us. And there's an opportunity cost to not doing so. Think about it this way—you can't spot every single person who is seriously struggling beneath the surface. So, be consistently kind and respectful to those whom you come into contact with. You could be saving a life by doing so—and not even realizing it at the time. Your routine act of kindness could change the trajectory of someone's day—or someone's life.

I remember a moment in life when my mom may have been proudest of me—and given that her nickname is "Stone Cold," it says a lot when she is willing to offer up a compliment.

It wasn't garnering international cheerleading awards. It wasn't graduating from college with honors or later from law school. And it wasn't getting elected to the US Senate in historic fashion.

It was a moment in sixth grade.

Mom got a call from my teacher. For a parent, that can be a nervous moment. *Is my child ok? Did my child do something wrong? Did we forget to sign something?*

But this was not one of those calls.

"Mrs. Boyd, I just wanted to tell you something. I've noticed it a few times now, and I feel like you should know. We've had a few new kids at school, and Katie has gone out of her way to sit with each of them at lunch. She makes sure they're included and that they're feeling welcome."

I didn't think much of it at the time. That's how my parents had raised me, and I was just trying to help my classmates feel comfortable, even if I had to go out of my comfort zone to do it. They were in a new environment, and I knew I would want someone to do the same for me if I was in their shoes.

To me, that kindness was a little thing—an ordinary thing that was done without giving it second thought. Yet, to those kids on the receiving end—and even the teacher watching as it happened, it made a real impact.

There is no greater success in life than helping the traditionally unseen feel seen. Make those rarely granted a voice feel heard. Offer belonging to the lonely. Lift up the forgotten—and show them that you remember them.

These can be hard things. Accomplishing them might take us out of our own comfort zones. But it is a sign of strength—and completely within our control—to answer this call.

CHAPTER 9

Water Your Plants and Your People

OVER TIME, how we treat people closely translates into our relationships with people.

Of course, treating someone well once or on occasion does not automatically mean your relationship with that person is strong. Relationships are like plants—they require constant nurturing. Again, intentionality is crucial.

If we're in the habit of treating people with kindness and respect, we're off to the right start in building healthy relationships. But we have to continually invest in their upkeep and growth.

One of the simplest, yet most important, aspects of this is showing up and truly being present.

Showing up is a critical component of all kinds of things in life. In politics, it is often said that decisions are made by those who show up—and that's true. In our careers, showing up and actually putting in the work is key. The same goes for our relationships.

There is something we will never be able to quantify about a person's willingness to be in the moment alongside us. So many times, that's exactly what we need—that's entirely what we really need. Because life is all over the place. It can be fun. It can be scary. It can be lonely. It can be comfortable. It can be hard. It can be anything and everything. But the people who are willing to be in the moment with us, no matter which moment it is, are few and far between.

It can take sacrifice to continually show up for people. Life is full of opportunity costs—showing up for someone likely means forgoing the chance to do something else with our time, energy, or resources. This is part of why showing up means so much in relationships. People know that you have to prioritize them enough to show up. Not showing up signals that something else was more important. If this becomes a pattern, they know where they stand.

That's not to say you have to show up every single time for each person in your life. That would be impossible.

This brings us to an unfortunate reality of life: we can't be all things to all people. And we shouldn't try.

It's natural to want to please people. It's normal to want to say "yes" when people ask us to do things. But overcommitting can be fatal for reputations and relationships.

I ran smack-dab into this harsh reality in college.

As the semesters passed, I had more and more on my plate. Class. SGA. Extracurricular organizations. My sorority. Teaching dance at a local studio to help pay for everything. And my friends and social life, of course.

I wanted to do it all. I refused to accept that I couldn't—that there was an opportunity cost associated with every piece of the pie I chose. My time was limited, so prioritizing one thing or even multiple things meant somewhere along the way I would run out of room for other things, even things I still wanted to do—and things

I had committed to do. I overextended myself, and that meant I wasn't able to show up for everyone who expected me to show up.

Even worse, it put me in situations where I couldn't keep my word. PaPa had told me when I was younger, "We're only as good as our word. Each and every one of us."

I originally thought at the time he tried to teach me that lesson that it was as simple as not lying. Yet, putting those words into practice is much more complicated, because life is complicated.

In college, there were many times when my friends would ask me if I wanted to do something, and I would enthusiastically respond, "Absolutely!"

"Let's do it. That sounds great."

In the moment, I meant what I said. I wasn't lying. I really wanted to do that thing.

However, when the time came, I had multiple other things going on that took priority. So, I couldn't show up for my friends. And I failed to keep my word.

Relationships are built on respect and kindness, but without a foundation of trust, they crumble.

Trust can be difficult enough to establish. There is no doubt, however, that the hardest thing to repair is trust.

Eventually, I lost my roommates' trust as a freshman in college because I repeatedly was not setting realistic expectations, I was not showing up for them, and I was not keeping my word as a result. Jamie and Elizabeth were two of my closest friends, but I was not treating them how they deserved to be treated—and I was not investing properly in our relationships. I took them for granted amid the hustle and bustle of life. This contributed to a real rift between us for almost a year. That was a tough time and an even harder lesson to learn.

There were other takeaways from learning to live with other people, too. First, everyone has their own idiosyncrasies and preferences. There are inherent challenges in getting to know your roommates and adjusting to how they live. Show people grace, put empathy into practice, and treat others with kindness and respect—even when you're not on the same page in a living situation. You also have to have self-awareness about your own quirks and understand that not everyone thinks like you or likes things exactly how you do. For example, I was terrible about not closing the liner and curtain after using the shower—until a suitemate later in college pointed it out to me.

Looking back, my fallout with my freshman roommates was also a study in the ramifications of passive-aggressiveness and not handling things on the front-end, as well. At the end of the day, there was not some big thing that punctured the hull of our relationships. There were a lot of unspoken things that individually were very minor—but we let these little things fester. We hid from confrontation and disagreement. And that snowballed into a big deal and something that seemed beyond repair at the time.

If we would have hit things head-on, we could have corrected things as they happened instead of letting small disputes compound over time. You can be direct with people while still being kind. Open, respectful dialogue is integral to healthy relationships of all types. It's natural to not want to hurt people's feelings or broach a touchy subject. However, having tough conversations in an intentional, constructive manner leads to the most productive outcomes in the long run.

I failed to follow this advice my first year in college. Jamie, Elizabeth, and I were supposed to live together again the coming year. We had committed to doing so in September of our freshman year—way ahead of sophomore year rolling around—because places to live fill up fast in Tuscaloosa. However, as our freshman year progressed, the situation slowly deteriorated to the point where I did not even know how to be in the same room with them, much less live with them another year. So, I quietly went and found myself a new place to live. I chose what was likely the *worst* possible way to handle it. My best self was missing in action.

I failed them. I failed myself. I failed our friendship.

It took about two years after that and Jamie being the bigger person to repair the damage. I will never forget her calling and asking me to come over to her apartment. We sat there on bar stools in front of her kitchen island.

"I need to forgive you. And I need to ask for your forgiveness," she told me.

That conversation lifted a weight off of our backs. It was honest. It was raw. It was healing.

Elizabeth and I reconciled a little bit later. We were finishing up lunch in Hoover after a Blackburn Symposium, and she realized I was looking for a ride back to Tuscaloosa and offered me one. That was a big step for her, and I knew it. While it took me until the Vance exit, probably about 30 minutes into the drive, to work up the nerve to truly talk about everything, I knew she was giving me my opportunity.

And we worked on rebuilding our relationships over the years. They became some of my closest friends again. And on January 3, 2023, both Jamie and Elizabeth were in the Senate gallery as I was sworn into office. There are relationships in life that are always worth fixing. And sometimes that is a hard thing. We could still be carrying the mental or emotional scars from what caused the schism in the first place, and sometimes they are sensitive to the touch. It's imperative that we seize second chances when they are presented—and be open-hearted to granting them ourselves.

I am so incredibly grateful that I was able to seize the second chance with these two women and their timeless friendships. There is a pit in my stomach when I think of what wouldn't have been if Jamie didn't have the courage to ask me to come to her apartment that day or if Elizabeth hadn't offered me a ride and given me 55 miles of driving to broach the topic the same way that Jamie broached it with me.

Forgiveness can be tough. Jamie taught me that sometimes it can be as important to forgive as it is to be forgiven. There are burdens in life that we didn't create and shouldn't have to carry. If you are carrying one of those burdens, sometimes forgiveness can allow you to set it down. Every story doesn't end like ours, but I do know that both forgiving and being forgiven can be restorative and liberating.

I am grateful for the grace those two young women gave a younger version of me. I'd like to think that I showed them grace, too. I think that's what allowed us to repair and rebuild.

Showing grace is not only a gift to those to whom you extend it—many times it is also a gift to yourself. It's a concept I learned growing up, but I had never really been forced to put it into practice. I knew the rule but not how to apply it in the real world. I ran into the same thing after law school. I learned the letter of the law in class, but the real understanding post-graduation is practical application of the law.

When I was younger, PaPa and my dad had both told me on several occasions that keeping your word is not optional. It matters. Treat it like it's mandatory.

People count on us. When you commit to doing something, people plan accordingly. They give up other opportunities and pass on other experiences. So don't give them false hope. Keep your word and show up when and where you say you're going to show up.

That's how I was raised. But in the midst of trying to navigate uncharted waters and juggle the demands of college, I failed to practice what I had been taught—what I knew to be right.

I took this failure and used it to shape me for the better moving forward. Now, I strive to always be intentional. I embrace being candid and direct. And if I say I'm going to be somewhere or do something, I'm going to follow through or die trying.

I also learned to handle as much as you can on the front-end of situations. My sophomore year, I lived in the basement of a house with my own bedroom, kitchen, bathroom, and washing machine. I had my own entrance and exit, so it wasn't really until junior year that I had an opportunity to put into practice the lessons I had learned from my freshman missteps.

Megan—or *Rooms*, as we fondly still refer to each other—and I moved into a small, shared space our junior year. We knew each other, but not terribly well, when we decided to live together. I didn't want to repeat the same mistakes from earlier in my college experience, so I got her to sit down with me on the front end. We talked through our own pet peeves, whether it be dirty clothes on the floor or old food sitting out on the desk. And we followed that up by talking through the best way to engage each other if there was something that was getting under our skin.

That was invaluable. It undoubtedly helped each of us know how the other preferred to be approached about a *hard thing*. Additionally, when we'd follow the other person's suggestion in how we address the issue—no matter how difficult the topic may be—you knew they were trying to be respectful because they were literally following the suggestion *you* gave them on how best to handle *you*. Both of us were bought in. With that came a sort of permission to bring things to the table. It allowed little things to be addressed before they became big things.

We also talked about the best way to help each other when we were stressed or seemed off. I have found asking this question and learning the answer to be one of the most important things in friendship. It is easy to be a friend in the highs of someone's life, but you really determine who your true friends are by seeing who supports you when you're down and struggling.

Some people like space—they want you to acknowledge it and then let them be. Others want you to sit with them and listen and actively help them work through it. Some people appreciate encouragement—while others find constant encouragement as annoying. Do you know what your friends need when they are facing hardship? Do you know what kind of support they actually crave? If you don't know, pay attention and learn. Or just ask them directly—and then actually listen to their response.

Watering your people is more than showing up when things are fun, easy, and convenient. It is being willing—and knowing how—to show up when it isn't. I am proud to say that *Rooms* and I lived together both junior and senior year. We have a unique bond and are still the dearest of friends to this day. We got a head start on friendship by talking about the hard things on the front end.

Relationships are like plants. Every plant needs something different to survive—different amounts of sunlight, different temperatures, *even* different amounts of water. If you treat all of them exactly the same, they all will not thrive. If you neglect them in certain ways, they will wither and eventually die. But if you understand what they need and nurture them, it will be incredibly rewarding to watch them flourish.

CHAPTER 10

Class Never Goes Out of Style

RELATIONSHIPS ARE BUILT ON TRUST and respect.

One thing that we must remember when I say this is that relationships are not contingent on agreeing with someone all the time—or even most of the time.

Anyone who thinks that it's possible to agree with someone 100% of the time has clearly never been married.

But whether the relationship is personal or professional in nature, it is ok to disagree with someone. It's normal to disagree with people.

What sets us apart is our ability to disagree agreeably.

This is something that used to be societally commonplace. But looking around at the world now, it seems to be going extinct—a development that's undoubtedly harming our society—and a large part of the root cause is social media and digital communication.

Working for Senator Shelby, I saw how professional relationships were built on trust, respect, and kindness on Capitol Hill—and how those well-formed relationships could lead to tough yet constructive conversations that ultimately produced meaningful results for the American people. One of Senator Shelby's closest friends during his service in Washington was Senator Patrick Leahy, a Democrat from Vermont. They came from polar opposite ends of the political spectrum. But that did not impact their ability to be friends and good colleagues.

That kind of across-the-aisle collegiality is becoming rarer. People would rather dunk on political opponents on Twitter than get to know each other as people.

However, there is no excuse for our own behavior to follow this trend. We are still completely in control of how we treat others.

Why is it that we view it as some strange phenomenon when people with different beliefs, perspectives, or backgrounds treat each other with kindness?

You don't have to agree with someone to respect them. That's a mentality I carry with me in the halls of the Capitol, and it's one with which I've tried to live my life.

The summer before my senior year of high school, I met Robert, who became one of my great friends in life. I appointed him as my executive chief of staff when I was elected as SGA president in college. We had different backgrounds, experiences, and perspectives, and when it comes to politics, we rarely agreed. But that didn't negatively affect our friendship.

I've found that differences in opinion among friends and among people who respect each other can make both parties stronger—and disagreements, if handled correctly, shouldn't weaken a relationship. Contrary perspectives are healthy. Hear them out and engage in constructive dialogue—and debate—to help inform and hone your own beliefs and positions. My friendship with Robert is a prime example of this.

Someone with whom you disagree is every bit as deserving of respect, kindness, and grace as someone with whom you agree. The Golden Rule does not have an exception for people who think or believe differently than us.

The same goes for how we handle adversarial situations in life, whether it is in sports, politics, or the race for a promotion at work. Even when we are competing against someone, it is vital that we be intentional about treating them well. It is the right thing to do, and you will reap the rewards in the long run if you do it.

Whether we have just succeeded or just failed, how we handle an outcome or result is just as important as that achievement or setback. People will likely remember how we acted in the aftermath—especially how we treated other people—longer than they will recall what we were reacting to.

Be gracious in defeat and humble in victory. I have had experience with both sides of this coin—especially the defeat part. How people handle both scenarios can either shine a light or cast a shadow on their character.

Do not take away from someone's win. If you come up short, evaluate yourself and how you can be better moving forward. Take responsibility and own what was under your control that went wrong. Have the humility to account for your mistakes. Then make a detailed plan to avoid a repeat result the next time around. No one is responsible for your success or failure but you.

I certainly have not always gotten this right, although I have tried in life's peaks and valleys. But one example of which I am particularly proud was how I handled winning at Girls State.

After being elected governor at Girls State, I asked the girl I ran against to be my chief of staff. I was impressed with her. She had done a phenomenal job, and I thought she deserved recognition for her hard work, poise, and knowledge of the issues.

At the end of the weeklong program, the Girls State governor gets to travel to the Capitol in Montgomery to meet the governor of Alabama. "It shouldn't just be me who gets this opportunity," I thought. So, I brought my new chief of staff with me. She had graciously accepted the role—and then the trip offer. We sat at the governor's conference table and talked with him over lunch.

Fast forward about 20 years, and I sat at the same table across from Governor Kay Ivey—who had been a speaker at my Girls State. I was now president and CEO of Alabama's business council. The room looked identical, only this time there were different people in the chairs. Life comes full circle.

A few years before that, I arrived at the Port of Mobile to take a tour as Senator Shelby's chief of staff. I got out of the car and there to greet me was that very person who ended up being my chief of staff at Girls State. Life comes full circle once again.

Wesley definitely experienced both the low points of defeat and the thrill of victory during his football career. At the University of Alabama, essentially his entire tenure was a masterclass on handling adversity with grace, class, and perseverance. His time with the Patriots would subsequently give him a view of both sides of the coin—and in exceptionally agonizing fashion.

The Patriots' 2007 season was one for the history books. They became the first team to win every regular season game since the NFL schedule was extended to 16 games. They did it in dominant fashion, too—their points scored per game averaged more than double that of their opponents. The playoffs went according to plan at first. The Patriots beat the Jaguars and then the Chargers, who had originally drafted Wesley. And then came that Super Bowl against the Giants.

The Patriots were the heavy favorites heading into that game in Glendale, Arizona. The game was tight throughout, and the Patriots led 7-3 heading into the fourth quarter. Then there were two lead changes. It was coming down to the wire.

The Giants, trailing 14-10, got the ball back on their own 17-yard line with 2:39 left in the game. Fueled by the now-infamous "Helmet Catch" and poised play by Eli Manning, they marched down the field and scored the winning touchdown with just 35 seconds left on the clock. The Patriots' dreams of joining the 1972 Dolphins in achieving a perfect season were dashed on the spot. Looking back, we probably should have taken it as an omen when the halftime performance was announced as Tom Petty and the Heartbreakers.

Wesley vividly remembers being in the Patriots' locker room right after the game. Players were devastated. Emotions were visceral. The chance to accomplish perfection—to carve their names into football immortality—had slipped through the team's fingers.

The room was silent. It was as if the oxygen had been sucked from it. And then Coach Belichick came in.

He took ownership. The loss was on him, he told the players.

"I didn't coach my best game. I didn't prepare like I should have."

Like Coach Saban does now in Tuscaloosa, Coach Belichick has a "24-hour rule." You get 24 hours to celebrate a victory or mourn a loss. And then you move on.

"Tomorrow, we get started with the offseason," Coach Belichick emphasized. "Let's use this feeling of defeat as fuel to improve.

Let's get better and put ourselves in the best possible position to win the next one."

Coach Belichick didn't complain about refereeing decisions. He didn't make excuses or deflect responsibility. And he didn't take away from the Giants win—they had played the game of their lives and deserved credit. He just got back to work and focused on controlling what he could control moving forward.

Wesley explains that this was pretty typical for Belichick after losses. When the Patriots lost, he didn't hide. Instead, he was vocal in public about the need for his coaching to be better next time out. He would talk about how the team as a whole could improve. He did not fixate on external factors outside their control. Conversely, when the Patriots did win it all, Coach would praise only his players for why the team came out victorious. The losses were on him, and the wins were credited to the players.

"No matter how complex the game plan and schemes, Bill had a way of boiling the game down to the foundational principles of success. 'Do your job' was a common refrain, and, 'Use every tool in your toolbox' was another," Wesley shares. "On that day, the Giants simply 'did their job' better than we did. The loss should always hurt, but there is no productive reason to not hold your head high and be intent on becoming better for the experience."

This is the type of leadership mentality and behavior that has made Coach Belichick an all-time great. How you handle both victory and defeat separates the best from the rest.

And win or lose, how we treat people matters.

We also shouldn't forget that not everything in life is a competition. For those areas that are a contest, we shouldn't be ashamed to win when we're being our best selves. Winning—when earned—is gratifying. And, if you're anything like me, avoiding the agony of defeat is even more of a motivator.

But we can also be tempted to treat situations that are not a zero-sum game as win-lose. In my experience, women are even more prone to this kind of unhealthy mentality, especially in professional settings. Because opportunities have historically been more limited for women in many fields, we mistakenly think of fellow women in the workplace as competitors rather than colleagues. However, we don't need to—and we very much shouldn't—step over one another while trying to ascend career ladders. When I have the opportunity to talk with young women, I remind them that you want to get somewhere on merit, not meanness. That type of behavior is self-perpetuating and self-defeating.

When we reach the pinnacle of a particular field—no matter whether it is academic, professional, athletic, extracurricular, or anything in between—our journey is not complete. Because the true measurement of success is not our ability to merely reach the final destination—but instead the manner in which we got there and how many others we are able to help flourish along the way.

Others' successes do not make us a failure, and others' failures do not make us a success. Reach back and help others behind you climb as you rise. Their achievements do not diminish yours—they add to them.

Unfortunately, I have witnessed my fair share of people in various work settings who fall into the trap of believing that they need to bring others down to rise themselves. I've seen both colleagues and supervisors guilty of this. Don't be that person. That person never wins in the end. And remember—you'll never be able to buy class.

Real character and strength come from empowering—not undercutting or sidelining—those around you. This is mutually beneficial. And it's what we're called to do.

CHAPTER 11

Find Your Walking Group

THROUGHOUT LIFE'S PLETHORA OF STAGES, each of us needs our core group of people whom we can always count on. Whether it's celebrating the good times or having each other's backs during the most turbulent of phases, those select people that will steadfastly ride the rollercoaster of life—no matter how high or low it goes—are truly special and should be cherished.

I think of this as our "walking group" in life. That probably shows the chapter of life that I'm in right now.

Every weekday morning at 5:00 am, I get up and head to meet up with my literal walking group—a group of five dear friends who live nearby. All six of us are moms of school-aged kids. At 5:15, we begin walking. As we walk, we discuss things happening in our lives and that are on our minds. We bounce things off of each other. We listen. We offer each other support and advice. We're present for one another. At that time of the morning, there is a peace that we rarely find in life anymore. There is no distraction of text messages, an urgent email from work, or a need to cut it short for a carpool pick up. By 6:15, we're home in time to wake up the kids and get them ready for school.

These women were kind enough to let me join them when I moved back to Montgomery several years ago and was really searching for my place. When the Senate is out of session and I'm home in Alabama, one of the things I look forward to most is joining my walking group. Whether we are physically together walking every morning or not, however, we can count on each other. These are the kind of friends who are always just a phone call or a text away. They'll drop anything and come running when you need it.

We help run carpool for each other when work obligations call. We show up with food after a surgery or illness. We pray for the healing of a child and walk with each other as we search for solutions. We celebrate our grandparents—centenarians and the ones that are almost there—and grieve together those we have lost. And many times, we find a way to do what we know the person needs, even when they haven't asked. We make sure that both in life and on the roads of our community, we *never* have to walk alone.

Your walking group doesn't have to actually walk, of course. Your support group will look different as your life stages shift. But the one constant is that you need this kind of close friend group who you can always rely on.

I was uniquely blessed with three built-in members of my walking group from a young age—my sisters. They have always been my teammates in life. We build each other up and give straight talk when it is needed. We inspire, encourage, and love each other through life's ups and downs. We have an unbreakable bond that not all siblings enjoy. We learned early on to have each other's backs and have never forgotten how important that is.

Growing up, my group also consisted of friends like Sally and Katie. Sally and I are six days apart, and with our parents being the best of friends, we have proudly claimed that title since birth. She is smart, determined, frank, and faithful. She loves the Lord and our hometown, Enterprise. So does Katie. She and I became best friends at Dauphin. Probably one of the most challenging times not only to become but to actually *be* my friend. And there she was with unwavering loyalty and a quick dismissal of any attempt to undermine our friendship. She is real, honest, kind, and direct. They are both just flat-out good people. They were rocks throughout the roughest of times. They are still those kinds of friends—the type of people who will always be there for you, regardless of physical proximity or life's changes.

In college, I met two more of my lifelong walking group members—Carlie and Jamie. Talk about people who always show up, no matter the distance or hurdles.

From our sophomore year to DC internships and our weddings to family vacations, it has been an honor to stand by Carlie's side and to have her stand by mine. Her boldness, love for life, intellect, and grit are contagious. She is unafraid to tackle hard things. She is loyal and she is fierce—and every room is immediately brighter once she walks through the door. Carlie flew right up to see me when Bennett was born. And the night before I announced my US Senate candidacy in 2021, Carlie was literally at my doorstep—and without me saying a word. She knew I needed her, so she showed up.

Even while being pregnant with her seventh child, there was no campaign stop in Jamie's hometown that she didn't make. From hosting an event at her home to being at the election night party with baby Henry in tow, she has prayed with me and encouraged me throughout life's ups and downs. Her walk with the Lord inspires me, along with her kind heart and her ability to deal with tough things head-on. And her sheer presence is always a joyful reminder that no matter what you have going on in life, you make time for those you love.

It's so important to have those friendships. But you can't have them without doing your part. They are built and earned. They don't just materialize out of thin air.

There's always a give-and-take nature to friendships. How much you put into them and how much you need out of them will fluctuate over time. You will find yourself in stages of life when you can give more—and when more is needed from you. Then there will be the intervals in which you need more from them.

In order to have the kind of friends you want in life, you have to *be* the kind of friend you want. Invest in your relationships with intentionality and generosity.

The manner in which we are able to invest in our friendships will naturally vary over the years as well. Take my walking group, for example. Our friend group has taken on this form because of where we all are in life—as moms and as people in general. Walking early in the morning is a function of the realities and constraints of our busy schedules. And ultimately, the time together is much less about the walking than it is about the conversation.

I had a similar support group in law school as well. No surprise here, but how we gathered and showed up for one another centered around time studying together. But these relationships were more than creating outlines and flash cards. These friends were there at our house—rather, what was left of it—after the April 27, 2011, tornado. And after graduation, we have consistently been there for each other, whether it be in some of life's most challenging situations, like the tragedy of losing ones we love, or to celebrate each other's wedding or the birth of a child. We wouldn't have it any other way. And no matter how much time goes by between phone calls, we pick *right* back up where we left off.

Carving out time for your relationships is critical, no matter where you are in life. How this materializes in high school or college will look different than how it fits into life with a growing family or in retirement. Lean into what uniquely works amid your personal and professional priorities and responsibilities. Finding this time for friends and making it work for everyone involved can be challenging, but it is always worth it. Show up for your people.

It is also important to remember that in some of our most challenging moments in life, we don't know how to ask or even what we need to ask for. I learned this after the tornado. I didn't want to inconvenience anyone and wasn't quite sure what we needed even if I did. But I needed help, I needed my people. It doesn't have to be a big gesture. In fact, it can be small. But the bottom line is that if someone you know is dealing with one of life's hurdles, find a way to show up.

In choosing or finding your walking group and making these crucial investments, you also need to be deliberate about surrounding yourself with the right people. Relationships can fill your cup, but they can also drain it. We tend to absorb personality traits, habits, and behaviors from those we spend the most time with. So, pick people who are uplifting, who empower you—and who hold you accountable when you need it. They call them "blind spots" for a reason. In life, we occasionally need other people's help to see things clearly. And make sure you're doing the same in return.

Wesley likes to say, "Show me your five closest friends, and I'll show you where you'll be in five years."

Pick people who make you the best version of yourself—and in being your best, help others reach their full potential.

This is not just important in personal relationships. I have benefited throughout my career from having a dedicated professional support group, too. In recent years, it has been professional women of a similar age. Each of us has climbed the ladder in our respective fields. We have earned each other's trust—which is easier said than done. We come from various arenas, but we all understand that trust is hard to earn and easy to lose.

We guard our time together and have created a space in which we can be candid, bounce things off of each other, vent when needed, pick each other's brains, and ultimately grow together. We discuss challenging bosses, direct reports, and the work-life balance—because while we all have demanding jobs, we know the importance of family. And we've also become each other's champions. Many times, women don't support other women, especially in professional spaces. I'm glad to say we've broken that mold—and I hope that we can set a new standard.

It is clear that no matter what phase of life, elementary school until now, I have benefitted from an incredible walking group—including many wonderful friends unnamed in these pages. I am truly grateful for each and every one of them and sincerely could not have done life without them. And it is not lost on me that no one gets anywhere alone.

Look for the people in your life who are just as willing to walk alongside you when the going gets tough as they are eager to celebrate the good times with you. These are your people.

I sure hope you find your walking group—I certainly would not be here without mine.

CHAPTER 12

Empowerment Comes in All Shapes and Sizes

EACH ONE OF US IS CALLED to be the best version of ourselves. But none of us can attain that goal alone. The influence and impact of others is essential to our lifelong development. Likewise, we have a central role to play in helping others learn and prosper throughout life. These dynamics are symbiotic and cyclical.

Acts of empowerment can come in all shapes and sizes. Sometimes, empowerment comes through the constant example of core role models in our lives. Other times, empowerment comes in a fleeting, otherwise ordinary interaction.

I'll never forget those who empowered me. There have been people in every season of life without whom I would not be here today.

Some of these people were closer to me than others. There, of course, were family and friends. Others were educators, classmates, colleagues, and bosses. But some were people I barely knew—they probably thought of their actions as small, but they had a big impact on me, nonetheless.

I think of the challenging times first.

There was junior high school and high school. By 10th grade, the weight of some kids' cruelty was really wearing heavily on me. I was struggling and feeling isolated, despite the loving support of family and close friends. That was also my first year on the varsity cheerleading squad. It was a pretty lonely experience, except for two of the seniors—Rebekah and Emily—who took me under their wing, for which I am still grateful to this day. Little things made the biggest difference, like them finding me at break to make sure I had someone to stand with or them offering me a ride home after practice. I don't know how I would have gotten through that year without them—their grace and their kindness.

Of course, there was also the aftermath of the tornado in law school. This goes back to three straightforward words: just show up. After the devastation, I didn't know much of anything. I had no clue what I needed—I didn't even have an immediate idea of what I had left. All I knew was that I needed my people to show up. And they did. *Be a person who shows up*, even when it isn't easy or convenient.

Acts of empowerment, like kindness, can be small but pack a powerful punch. I've found that the most empowering individuals find ways to empower others without people even realizing it is happening in the moment. It can happen in a flash but last a lifetime.

I think back to Mrs. Metcalf, my first-grade teacher. She had this old popcorn maker on a table by her desk to the side of the room. Friday afternoons in her class were a real treat. She'd fire that machine up, and the popcorn smell soon filled the entire room. Mrs. Metcalf appointed me as her popcorn helper. That was a real honor in itself. I'd serve it to my classmates in those little paper bags. But I have never forgotten one Friday in particular. After I did my service, she told me that I was special. Until that moment, I hadn't felt special. But she empowered me. She continued to tell me that *anything* was possible throughout my entire life. She believed more was possible for me and wanted me to believe it, too. Because of her, I did believe. And I achieved.

Mrs. Metcalf actually made a video for me during my campaign for the Senate in 2022. She recounted how she told me all those years ago that she believed I would be the first female President of the United States. Now even my first-grade self knew that to be a bit of a stretch, but what it did was spark a confidence inside me. I can't quite explain it, but if this woman believed I was capable of *that*, then I was certainly capable of more than I assumed. It is amazing what a difference it can make when someone believes in you and takes the time to express it.

Her funeral was held a few months before the General Election. I wish I could have told her after stepping onto the floor for the first time as a US Senator that her empowering that little first grader decades earlier made the moment possible. No matter how young a child is, empowering words—and the confidence that is instilled by them—stick with that person throughout life.

Wesley has a similar memory of a teacher empowering him in an enduring way. His ninth-grade geometry teacher, Mrs. Boozer, helped make Wesley feel like the highest levels of academic achievement were possible for him. He had just been in the hospital with a staph infection (induced by a football injury) and missed a few weeks of school as a result. When he returned to class, there were a few tests that had piled up. He needed to take them and do well. To this day, he remembers Mrs. Boozer's reaction to him excelling on that first test after he got back. She was effusive in telling Wesley how well he had done—and how sharp he was.

"Looking back, I don't even know if anything I did on that test *was* special—but she made me feel like I hung the moon," Wesley reflects.

At that time in his life, no one had really yet made him feel smart. She believed in him and was vocal about how impressed she was by him. He set out to prove her right—and he did throughout his undergraduate and graduate successes. He already unknowingly had the smarts, but he needed to believe in what was possible to unlock their use.

Unfortunately, the possibilities of empowerment can go the other way, too. People's belief in themselves can be crushed by the actions of others, especially with young people. Before the empowerment of Mrs. Boozer, Wesley's confidence was stifled by a teacher in seventh grade. He was sitting in class when the call came over the intercom for the math team to report to the gym and get their group photo made for the yearbook. Wesley, who was on the team and quite good at math, got up to head to the picture. But the teacher told him to take his seat.

"She told me to sit down," Wesley says, now with a bemused chuckle. "There's no way I could be on the math team. You know, people try to put you in a box. I was a football player and rambunctious. But I was also on the math team. You can be all of those things at the same time."

This also goes to show how true the old saying is: "Don't judge a book by its cover."

So, before you are quick to judge, dismiss, or make a comment, think about your words or actions. You have the ability to motivate others—in a positive or negative direction. And that persuasive power can be tremendous.

Later in life, Wesley got to see a master motivator at work in Coach Belichick. Wesley can still picture Coach's office and his books, which are mostly volumes on psychology.

One of Coach Belichick's greatest achievements, Wesley contends, is how he empowered and motivated Randy Moss. When the star receiver arrived in New England in 2007, he was coming off of drama-filled stints with the Vikings and the Raiders. There was no question about his talent, but many believed that he had garnered a reputation for being more trouble off the field than he was worth on the field at that point in his career.

Early in Randy's tenure with the Patriots, the players were gathered in the team meeting room, which consisted of an auditorium-style seating arrangement. Players were grouped up by position, with Wesley and the rest of the offensive lineman in the row right in front of Randy and the other receivers. Coach Belichick walked in, took his place at the head of the room, and began flipping through newspaper articles as he addressed the team.

"Look at all of these," Wesley retells Coach Belichick saying. "*Washington Post. New York Post. New York Times.* I think the *National Enquirer* is in this stack somewhere. And they're all saying the same thing. They say Randy Moss is going to be a distraction. They say he's going to cause us a problem. They say he's going to ruin the Patriots' locker room."

At this point, Coach Belichick tossed the papers to the ground.

"Now, guys, Randy has been the best teammate we've had," he continued. "He's been great in the locker room. He's been great on the field. Everything that we've asked him to do, he's done it."

Coach Belichick then turned directly to the man in the spotlight.

"Randy, you're going to be nothing but a great teammate, and we're not going to have any problems out of you, right?"

Randy didn't flinch. He confidently pledged that he wouldn't let the team down.

Wesley remarks, "And he kept his word. I think a large part of that was Coach Belichick showing Randy that he believed in him in front of the entire team. That motivated him to not let Coach down. He was a great teammate the entire time I played with him."

The Patriots organization thrived on that kind of culture. And it wasn't just Coach Belichick who led the charge.

The first moments of Wesley's time as a Patriot aren't something that he has ever forgotten.

He had just gotten off of a red-eye flight from San Diego after being cut from the Chargers and picked up by New England. Here he was, a rookie scrambling to make the roster, who had just finished a plane ride and the self-examination that came along with those silent hours. He went straight from the airport to the Patriots locker room so he could get ready for practice.

"One of the first people to introduce themselves, almost immediately, was Tom Brady," Wesley advises. "He said, 'Hey, Wes. I'm Tom Brady. I'm glad you're here, and I'm glad you're blocking for me.'"

Wesley laughs telling the story. "Yep, you're Tom Brady. You've won three Super Bowls. I had half a mind to ask for his autograph."

But that interaction, which was a small and ordinary thing, made all the difference for Wesley. He immediately felt welcome and empowered to do his job. And he was motivated not to let Tom down.

Empowered people empower others. Not everyone will be Tom Brady—or the Tom Brady of teachers, like Mrs. Metcalf. But we all have the ability to empower others—and be empowered by others—in our daily behavior and throughout life's journey.

FIND A MENTOR, BE A MENTOR

In working to be empowered and empowering in our lives, it is important that we all find a mentor and be a mentor. Always remember this: you're never too old to have a mentor, and you're never too young to be a mentor. We need role models to follow, but also need to model the way for others to follow.

I have been fortunate from an early age to have mentors who helped me learn foundational values, lessons, and skills—who have helped me strive to be my best and to continue raising the bar of what constitutes my best. The names mentioned in this book certainly aren't all inclusive.

We can't discount the importance of people in our lives who have more wisdom, unique experiences, and different perspectives than us. Some of these people will come into our lives in a way we can't control—like parents or other relatives. But for others, God places them in our path, and we then need to do our part in building a fruitful relationship with them.

Some of my earliest mentors were family. My parents. My grandparents. There were distinctive, irreplaceable things I gleaned from each one. But across the board, their respective examples all accomplished the same thing—they empowered me.

My mom and my dad constantly exemplified hard work, selflessness, and sacrifice. The intensity of Mom's daily routine, juggling parenthood and being a small business owner, was extraordinary. She rarely got a minute to even stop moving. I remember sometimes she would pick us up from school on Friday, and we would head straight to Lake Seminole in Georgia to visit her parents—Grandmomma and Granddaddy to me. During the week, my sisters and I would change in the car on the way to the dance studio every day. There would be enough clothes in the back by Friday afternoon that she could wash them when we got there—so she didn't have to pack.

At Lake Seminole, we would play outside and not be allowed to come back in until suppertime. Grandmomma believed that you should only have to be told something once. If we didn't mind her, she would pull out the switch. There were many times my cousin and I would have to go "pick the switch," which she kept on top of the refrigerator. However, it rarely had to be used—if ever—because its sheer presence was enough to get the job done. We played cards. Grandmomma taught my sisters and me Progressive Rummy, her card game of choice. We, in turn, taught our friends as we grew older. Progressive Rummy also became a family tradition. We even have a tournament during Christmas, and the winner gets the honor of their name being displayed on the plaque that still hangs in my grandparents' kitchen. It's right next to the sign that says, "This ain't no Holiday Inn." By that, Grandmomma meant, "Get it yourself, wash your dishes, and pick up your own trash."

My mom was born in Vicksburg, Mississippi, and her family is from Opp, Alabama—a city in Covington County known for hosting the annual Rattlesnake Rodeo. Mom was proud of her blue-collar upbringing. She was raised in Enterprise starting from the age of five and was taught to appreciate the important things in life. Granddaddy was in the Coast Guard before they moved back to the Wiregrass. Granddaddy and Grandmomma bought a store called Bill's Superette that was part gas station, part meat market, and part grocery on Ozark Highway in Enterprise. They ran it until my mom graduated from high school. That's when Granddaddy embarked on a career with Flowers Baking Company. Over the years he worked his way up from running bread routes to vice president through his sheer work ethic and determination. He eventually moved to the headquarters location in Thomasville, Georgia—above the Florida panhandle near Lake Seminole. Granddaddy probably would have risen to president of his respective bakery at Flowers, if not for the accident.

I still remember when it happened and Mom found out. I was very young at the time. Granddaddy was on a company hunting outing. Now, he did not like horses and avoided them whenever possible. But they were on an expansive property, and the buggy that usually transported people around who didn't want to ride a horse was broken that day. So, he had to ride a horse that one time. And that one time he had to ride a horse, it got spooked, reared back, and landed right on his pelvis with all of its weight.

It crushed him from the waist down. Doctors told him he may never walk again, and he was bedbound in the hospital for the next three months. However, he never gave up. He fought through the adversity, rehabbed intensively, and regained the ability to walk. Doctors thought it would be impossible, but he was dogged in his belief that he would prove them wrong. And he did.

For me, that was really inspiring to witness as a young person. It also put things in perspective. Here he was from a working-class background, someone who was right on the cusp of career achievements he would have thought were totally unattainable when he was growing up. Then, tragedy struck—and his life was flipped upside down. Despite being able to walk again, the injury left him with lifelong, severe nerve damage and pain in his leg and lower body. He has been unable to sit down normally since the accident because of the excruciating pain. He has to lie down or sit on his side at all times. But instead of complaining, he has persevered. Talk about grit. Every time I struggled with adversity in life, I thought about how Granddaddy has handled his—with strength and resolve. With willpower and heart. This always helps give me that extra boost to push through whatever life throws my way.

Grandmomma was another exemplar of fortitude. She was married at age 17 before she could graduate high school and quickly had five children. She was a worker bee at heart. Grandmomma worked just about any honest job she could get to help provide for her family while juggling the demands and stress of being a mother to her handful of kids. When they were a little older, she then took the time to get her GED and worked at H&R Block.

She was always up for an adventure, too. Grandmomma accompanied us on many of the dance trips that I think back on with the fondest memories. She made the cheerleading trip to Australia with me, as well. I'll never forget that one. And one of the most fun trips was the time my entire dance team took the train all the way up to New York City. We played cards for hours, namely Grandmomma's trademark Progressive Rummy. We also played Spades. We played MASH. The best part of the entire experience, though, was making our big entrance right into Grand Central Station. It gave us a sense of wonder and accomplishment before we even took the competition stage. And Grandmomma was right there with me.

It was April 2010 when she was diagnosed with cancer and given a three-month prognosis to live. She was determined to visit all of her grandchildren in her final weeks. My mom drove her around to see us where we were. They got to Tuscaloosa when Ridgeway was just weeks old. I'm still so glad she was able to meet her great-grandson. She brought Raggedy Ann dolls for both Bennett and Ridgeway. Bennett immediately began sleeping with hers every night.

Christmas was always a big deal for our family growing up, especially for Grandmomma. She loved gathering with her children and grandchildren every December. However, she knew she was not going to make it to the end of her last year. So, we moved the Donaldson family Christmas up to the summer in 2010 for her. It was a wonderful family celebration. We laughed, rejoiced, reminisced, and cried together. Before we left, Grandmomma wanted to leave us all with one thing—she said she was ready to meet her Savior, but first she wanted to make sure that we all had a personal relationship with Jesus Christ. She had my uncle, who is a preacher, discuss it with everyone. It was the most important thing to her, and that example laid down the gauntlet for our entire family to follow. It empowered us and reminded us to keep our eyes on the Lord.

MaMa has quite the story, too. After she graduated high school, World War II was raging. She wanted to serve our nation overseas, but women weren't allowed to enlist in combat roles at that time in our history. So, she embarked on a path to serve another way—becoming a nurse. It was 1943 when she enrolled at what was Hillman Hospital's School of Nursing. While she was studying there, it became Jefferson-Hillman, and today it is at the center of the University of Alabama at Birmingham's medical campus. MaMa was prepared to be shipped out to Europe; however, the war ended before she graduated. So, she moved to Enterprise upon earning her degree and began her nursing career. She would later become a Labor and Delivery nurse until she retired.

I think both sets of my grandparents typified their generation, which was rooted in unselfish service to our nation. They personified JFK's words, "Ask not what your country can do for you—ask what you can do for your country." That's the mindset that we need to get back to as a nation.

Unfortunately, the narrative has flipped in modern times. People have taken on a mentality of "What can you do for me?" My four grandparents helped teach their families that life isn't all about us. There is a greater purpose and a higher calling to which we all must answer and work in the service of. We all have a responsibility to put our God, our family, our friends, and our country above our own self interests. That service to our nation can take on many ways, shapes, and forms. For my grandfathers, it was military service. For other members of my family, it has been law enforcement or serving as a firefighter. For me, it is public service. You don't have to wear a uniform or hold elected office to serve. But each of my grandparents showed me by example that it is incumbent on each and every one of us to do better, to be better, and to leave things better than we found them. They modeled the way and empowered me as a result.

Both my dad and my mom learned the concept of service and

sacrifice from their respective parents, and I marveled at seeing them put these morals into practice throughout my adolescence. For his part, Dad worked tirelessly at least six days a week at the store, and then seven if he had a funeral to work on Sunday at the family cemetery. Because he had to work, he wasn't able to make all of our competitions and extracurricular events. He would always say, "I am so proud of y'all and wish I could be there, but someone has to pay for this." Watching him and my mom sacrifice so that we could have opportunity and enjoy childhood has forever stuck with me.

I also got a front-row seat to his work ethic and integrity from a young age. Beginning in kindergarten, I was working in Dad's hardware store. I started with inventory. I moved on to counting nuts and bolts—or, as my dad still corrects me, "The proper term is fasteners." I cleaned the shelves, and, *boy*, were they gross. Next, it was time to sweep up the back room where they rigged the boats. I would even count the coin drawer. Little did I know that my dad was quietly reinforcing things I learned at school and honing life skills the whole time.

Eventually, I got "promoted." I would answer the phone.

"Boyd's Marine. How may I direct your call?" I felt like a real grown-up saying that.

And I even helped to review receipts and "check the books." I received little pay but loved the ice-cold bottled Coke at the end of a hard day's work.

However, when I got into second grade, I wanted to branch out and work outside the hardware store. While I continued working with my dad on and off, I wanted new challenges.

One day, I got dressed in my Sunday best and asked Mom

to take me to Kids Korner, a local children's clothing store in Enterprise. I went right up to the owner and asked her for a job. I was blunt—I talked about how I made 50 cents an hour working for my dad. I was worth more than that, I told her. When I got a little older, I worked at Strickland Jewelers, too. Both places empowered me and inspired me to be my best. I learned, I grew, and I still cherish the days working at those Wiregrass small businesses.

Dad imparted to me the realities of running a family-owned small business, especially one in a tight-knit community like ours. When your name is on the line—and it always is when your family owns a small business—it makes a significant difference. There is a palpable pride and intentionality that you put into every detail of how your business operates. At the end of the day, human nature dictates that this personal touch is simply not there with big-box stores, when upper management and ownership are time zones removed and when their own families' livelihoods don't hinge on what happens inside those walls 24/7. That is why I believe the preservation of the local family business, the small business, is so critically important to the continued success of our great nation. It's something that was ingrained in me as a child and that I never lost sight of. I took that belief and that passion with me into my professional career, first as an attorney, then as Senator Shelby's chief of staff, as head of Alabama's business council, and now in the US Senate.

It's also inspiring to watch my sister, Janie, follow in Dad's footsteps now as she runs her own small business.

I had to find a slightly unorthodox way to carve out time to spend with my dad as he worked to run his small businesses and as my afterschool activities and weekend demands increased.

Thinking back, it was actually a pretty similar strategy to my walking group timeframe now.

When I got old enough, I would go to the local Gold's Gym with Dad most weekday mornings. This would have been in high school. We'd get up at 5:00 am and head to work out. I'd be so tired afterward. But the time with my dad made it well worth it. We would talk during the car rides there and then back home. Now, when I'm working out in the Senate gym the mornings when I'm in Washington, I think of those memories with Dad.

Even when it wasn't a trip to the gym, car rides became my go-to outlet to spend quality time with him. We would go to get a coffee or just ride around town to see what was happening. Sometimes, I would sit in his study with him. I can still picture a time period when he had an old pinball machine in there. Then there was his phonograph in the corner. I hear "Sgt. Pepper's Lonely Hearts Club Band" when I think of that record player and that treasured time with my dad.

Dad's parents, MaMa and PaPa, taught me more than I can remember. Those Sunday mornings and afternoons undoubtedly helped shape me into who I am today. Their lessons were foundational and continual—they empowered me throughout life.

We lost PaPa in 2016. To this day, MaMa at 98 years young still lives by herself at their home in Enterprise. She was so proud to fill in the bubble next to my name on her ballot three times in 2022—once each for the primary, runoff, and general elections. I told her that it was because of her and PaPa that the achievement was possible for me. They inspired me to dream and empowered me to achieve that dream. It was because of them that I first realized that your circumstances, your "pedigree" on paper, and your zip code do not take you out of the game. Then, they helped equip me with the tools needed to seize the opportunities that life offered.

On January 3, 2023, I was sworn into the Senate on two bibles—one each for Bennett and Ridgeway to keep. One was PaPa's. And the other was the bible my family gave me when I completed my First Communion.

There is a common thread that runs through my life's mentors. Whether they were immediate family or people I met along the way, I was blessed with Christian role models who truly lived their faith and helped others do the same through both their example and their counsel.

Another example of this is Ms. Jenny, who co-owned the studio with my mom and taught me dance growing up. She is deeply steeped in her faith and still texts me bible verses or devotions every day.

Or take my Uncle Mike. He is really why I wanted to be a doctor growing up. He is an otolaryngologist—an ENT doctor and surgeon—in Enterprise. I shadowed him on and off during summers in junior high through high school. That experience not only got me interested in medicine as an avenue to serve others, but I also got to see how he ministered to others through his practice. I remember the praise and worship music in his surgery center. He had bibles and devotionals in the waiting area for patients and their loved ones. That example is why I now keep a bible in the lobby of my Senate office in Washington for constituents and visitors. Uncle Mike is someone who embodies the values of faith, family, and freedom that make the Wiregrass such a special place.

I also saw how he treated people with respect and compassion. He always extended a gracious hand to the men and women in the community who served at Fort Rucker. He and Aunt Pam opened their home for everything from Bible studies for soldiers to renowned Alabama cook Brenda Gannt making homemade biscuits for the area's military personnel and families. And a piece of trivia about Uncle Mike—he was one of eight pallbearers at Coach Paul "Bear" Bryant's funeral. It was the first funeral he ever attended.

I actually introduced Wesley to Uncle Mike while we were in college, and he became a mentor to Wesley, too. Wesley says Uncle Mike's advice was particularly useful because he had essentially walked in Wesley's shoes before. Like Wesley, Uncle Mike played offensive line for the Crimson Tide. He was playing at the University of Alabama when Coach Bryant died in 1983.

"He knew what I was dealing with and had seen some of the potential traps I had to navigate around," Wesley reflects. "He really offered a no-judgment zone no matter what I was going through. He set an example of how I could handle everything thrown my way as a Christian young man—and later in life as a Christian husband and father."

Something Uncle Mike absorbed from his days playing for Coach Bryant was the importance of having and maintaining standards of excellence. He cautioned that you can never compromise on excellence, because as soon as you start compromising on that, you've just lowered your standards. From there, your standards' momentum would continue downward.

"Coach Bryant was very much about preparation," Uncle Mike explained in a 2020 interview with the Crimson Tide Foundation. "He was the first person to really stress to me that it doesn't matter on Saturdays. Everybody wants to win on Saturdays. He talked about what we did all the rest of the time; that's how you earn the right to be there on Saturday."

Uncle Mike is also someone who modeled unconditional love throughout his life. His youngest son, my precious cousin Parker, was born with special needs that presented serious health challenges during his inspiring 12-and-a-half years on Earth. He was never able to walk or talk, and he was dependent on a feeding tube, oxygen later in life, and was home on a ventilator his final year-and-a-half. While Parker may have been inaudible to the outside world, his heart and courage spoke to everyone who met him. Their entire family walked through life's difficulties with strength and grace while demonstrating true character and faith. It also put into practice something that Uncle Mike outlines Coach Bryant used to talk about.

"Life doesn't always deal fair hands to everybody, but you do what you do. You step up and do the right thing, and you do it well," Uncle Mike narrates Coach Bryant saying.

I met another lifelong mentor, Dr. Cathy Randall, when I was at Girls State as a rising senior in high school. She has been integrally involved in the program for decades—going back to when she was elected as president of Girls Nation when she was in high school. She was an incredible source of wisdom and inspiration when I was going through Girls State, and we stayed in touch as my freshman year of college drew closer.

Her distinguished résumé in business and civic leadership was lengthy. At the time, Dr. Randall led the Computer Based Honors Program at the University of Alabama, so she became a go-to source of insight and guidance the moment I stepped foot on campus. Anyone who has ever met Dr. Randall can affirm that she radiates character, class, and grace. Whether it was SGA, my sorority, academics, or life in general, she and the Girls State family have helped me steer through some really challenging times and encouraged me at the moments I needed it most. For example, I certainly wouldn't have had the nerve to run for SGA president without Dr. Randall's persistent confidence that I could achieve more than I thought I could. There is no doubt that I benefited immensely from her perspective and experiences. It was so important for me to have someone like this who understood what my strengths and weaknesses were and guided me on how to utilize my gifts and ultimately succeed.

I met another stalwart mentor in college, actually through Dr. Randall—Dr. Kathleen Cramer. Both are fiercely intelligent women who are shining lights for their faith and who helped me stand back up after my personal failures in college. Dr. Cramer dedicated her career to serving students at the University of Alabama. She taught me to be more interested in achieving the result than getting the credit. When I arrived in Tuscaloosa, she was an administrator in the division of Student Affairs. Dr. Cramer also deftly and graciously helped me traverse tough waters on campus, including my personal failures. She has been an unfaltering role model and a faithful friend to me since then, regardless of where in life I found myself.

I was blessed to find strong Christian women as mentors in college. Dee Mooty certainly fits that bill, as well. Ms. Dee is the mother of a good friend, Hal, who was active in SGA with me, and I met her when she came to Tuscaloosa one evening to have dinner with her son. It was an incredible blessing from God when He put Ms. Dee in my life. From that time, she has been someone whom

I can confide in and who never wavers in her kindness, selflessness, and love. Importantly, in every conversation, she points me toward Him. Life does have that tendency to come full circle—and our family now lives right down the street from her. She is always lightning quick to offer support, confidence, and cheer grounded in faith.

I met a few more mentors at the University of Alabama. I suppose there is a reason that my alma mater has trademarked the phrase, "Where Legends Are Made."

First, there is Dr. Robert Witt, who became president of the university in 2003. The month after he took his new post, I became the first SGA president to be elected during his tenure on campus. From the jump, he was truly a student-centered administrator. He authentically wanted to know what students thought and actively solicited that feedback. He is also a visionary. Dr. Witt launched a transformative plan for growth at the University of Alabama in just about every facet possible—academics, research, athletics, the campus facilities, you name it. This is something I got to witness not only as a student, but also when I returned to Tuscaloosa to work for the university following my stint as Senator Shelby's press secretary. Unquestionably, Dr. Witt has a razor-sharp business mind and executes plans with precision. He also has a gift for making people feel seen and valued—he did not look past or through people, he looked directly at them.

A few months after I met Dr. Witt, it came time for my summer internship in Senator Shelby's office as a rising senior in college. Following my graduation the next year, I served as his deputy press secretary and then press secretary. Talk about someone who thinks down the road and around the corner. Throughout his career, Senator Shelby epitomized the word "statesman." His legacy of service is that he changed what was possible for generations of Alabamians, including those yet to come. However, even with all he accomplished in office, I still think that his greatest feat was convincing Dr. Annette Shelby to marry him. She has been a vital driving force for his success, and she has been a trailblazer in her own professional right.

Dr. Shelby spent her career in academia, teaching at both the University of Alabama and Georgetown University for more than 30 years. She earned the distinction of being named the first tenured female professor and first female emerita professor at Georgetown University's McDonough School of Business. Dr. Shelby also directed Georgetown's undergraduate and graduate programs at Oxford University.

Having seen both Dr. and Senator Shelby in action, one of their keys to success that I gleaned was the amount they read—both for professional purposes and for pleasure. I would be shocked if anyone in recent memory checked out more books from the Library of Congress than the Shelbys. They love learning. They use every opportunity possible to capture knowledge. If Senator Shelby knew that he would be on the floor of the Senate for more than a few minutes at a time, he would bring a book to read. Usually, it was a history book. The speed at which he reads is remarkable, too. He can plow through most books in a single sitting.

In 2015, I was working for Butler Snow when I got a call from Senator Shelby. He was running for reelection in the 2016 cycle, and he requested my help. I did not hesitate. I took a leave of absence from the law firm and signed on as Senator Shelby's campaign communications director and deputy campaign manager.

More than a decade earlier, he gave me a chance that changed what was possible for me. And I wanted to make sure he had the opportunity to go out how he wanted to—and how I believed he should. That campaign quickly opened my eyes to how much American politics had changed in the several years I had been on the sidelines since leaving Washington. Most markedly, it was starkly apparent that social media had completely changed not only campaign messaging, but our societal discourse as a whole.

After a successful primary campaign victory in March 2016, Senator Shelby had one more ask of me. It was that following summer. I was outside doing some yard work when my phone began ringing. I looked at the screen and saw it was Senator Shelby calling. I tried to get Wesley to shut off the leaf blower, which was futile. So, I hustled away to try and be able to hear the voice on the other end of the phone as I answered.

Senator Shelby got right to the point: he wanted me to serve as his chief of staff. I knew this was an incredible honor but also a tremendous responsibility. Wesley shut off the leaf blower, and soon we were headed back to Washington. Serving in this role through late 2018 gave me another important opportunity to put lifelong lessons into practice, especially when it came to the fact that the way you treat people matters.

The task at hand made me really reflect on what type of leader I wanted to be, too. Throughout my career, I was blessed with role models. But I had also experienced my share of managers and supervisors who—on many days—exemplified how *not* to treat people.

When you finally get the chance to be in charge, I believe you have two choices: one, you can repeat the mistakes of those who have supervised you (after all, isn't that only fair), or, two, you can learn from their mistakes and treat others the way you wish you had been treated. The second pathway allows you to create an environment where those around you can both get their job done best and be their best as people.

Nobody gets anywhere alone. At least, nobody gets anywhere *good* alone. So, lead in a way that allows others to follow.

GIANTS AND GIFTS

My life is not the exception in this regard; it's the rule. Wesley's journey is filled with similar examples of mentors being integral to his development and success.

It started with his parents—Wesley's mom was a schoolteacher when he was growing up, and his dad was a small business owner. His dad's father, Wesley's paternal grandfather, was also a major influence on him. He was the one who ultimately gave him the advice that led him to choose the University of Alabama over the Florida Gators.

His grandfather's background characterized hard work. He was a sharecropper growing up in Blount County, Alabama. His dad before him had been a sharecropper, too. Wesley's grandfather was the oldest of five kids. When his dad died when he was a teenager, he packed up and headed off to a Civilian Conservation Corps work camp. He sent the money he earned back home to support his family. He and his unit started in Gatlinburg, Tennessee, and made it all the way to Oregon as they worked. When they reached their destination, they were lined up and told the shocking news. The Japanese had just bombed Pearl Harbor.

"We need you boys to suit up."

He immediately joined the US Navy and shipped out to Pearl Harbor before he even had time to go visit his family back in Alabama. He proceeded to serve on a battleship throughout World War II.

After the war, he moved to Holly Pond in Cullman County, where he raised a family, drove a school bus, and farmed.

"He did a little bit of everything," Wesley reminisces.

Wesley's dad went to Jacksonville State University, where he met Wesley's mom. Her family was originally from Boaz, Alabama, but she grew up as a military brat and graduated high school in Hawaii. Her dad was in the Air Force.

When Wesley's parents graduated from JSU, his dad took out a loan and bought a backhoe. Then a dump truck. His dad's business launched as a septic tank installation service. When he got into a motorcycle accident, Wesley's grandfather got involved in the business. He worked in septic tank installation pretty much until the day he died. Wesley's dad branched off into hauling coal for local miners.

"I remember going into coal pits with my family. And putting in septic tanks with Granddad," Wesley recalls. "That's where I learned work ethic. He would come get me at 4:30 in the morning, and we'd be out putting septic tanks in all day fueled by nothing but Mountain Dew and a Moon Pie."

Sometimes, he would get an RC Cola, Wesley added. His dad would take Wesley and his brothers in the dump truck to haul coal. They'd get to help shift gears as their dad drove. They'd typically transport the coal to end users in North Alabama, but they traveled across the Southeast over the years. It was a dangerous business, and Wesley's dad eventually transitioned into demolition work. Wesley remembers his first big demo job—tearing down the abandoned King Edward Cigar Plant in Cullman, which had employed about 500 people at its peak.

Like me, Wesley saw early and often what it means to be a small business owner. The leaps of faith you have to take to get things off the ground—and to grow, adapt, survive, and thrive. The hard work and doggedness. The sacrifice. The obligations that come with signing the back of a paycheck. As a child, Wesley walked outside to be driven to school one day. And that's when they realized their car had been repossessed. Making payroll and taking care of their employees came first. So, Wesley had to take the bus.

Wesley's dad also drove home the importance of faith and his church community from an early age. They were at church on Sunday mornings, Sunday evenings, and Wednesday evenings. Wesley says he can't remember watching a Super Bowl growing up because it conflicted with Sunday night church services. Their top priority was whatever their church had going on.

"I became a Christian when I was nine years old through Vacation Bible School," Wesley explains. "Dr. Edwin Hayes was our pastor. He spoke to us on the last day, and I had never been so moved in my life. My heart was pounding, and the presence of the Lord was so real to me. So, I prayed with Dr. Hayes and asked the Lord to come into my heart. It was an amazing thing when I invited the Lord into my life."

This upbringing served Wesley well as he headed to the University of Alabama, but the trappings of collegiate athletics at a major university is no cakewalk for anyone to navigate. Wesley says it was particularly daunting coming from a small town and immediately being tossed into a world filled with temptations and distractions. That's why he was so grateful to quickly meet yet another mentor who helped him grow in and live his faith at a precarious moment in his journey—Wayne Atcheson.

Wayne at the time was associate director of the Crimson Tide's football donor program and had served as the Athletics Department's Sports Information Director, with his time in Tuscaloosa dating back to 1983. Wayne was also the adviser to the campus's Fellowship of Christian Athletes chapter.

From the moment Wesley stepped on campus, Wayne was there to support and encourage him.

"He told me that he could see God working on me and working through me," Wesley recollects. "Mr. A worked hard to make sure I remained focused on my faith."

Wayne was a key part of Wesley's development as a Christian leader during his first few years in Tuscaloosa. Wayne left his post with the Tide in 2003—the year Wesley became president of the Fellowship of Christian Athletes at the University of Alabama—and was soon head of the Billy Graham Library, but not before he left an indelible mark on Wesley's heart and mind.

"Mr. A inspired me to work hard for the Kingdom," Wesley says.

Wayne stayed in touch with Wesley after he graduated and went to the NFL. Wayne routinely called to check in and sent texts and emails with words of encouragement and spiritual guidance. During Wesley's stint in San Diego, Wayne helped him get involved with the church of Pastor Rick Warren, the author of *The Purpose Driven Life*. And after Wesley hopped on a plane for New England, Wayne again connected him with a local faith program.

Even though Wesley's playing days are long over now, he continues to count Wayne as a mentor and dear friend. One of Wesley's favorite books is *Fifty Years of Crimson Tide Faith*, written by none other than Wayne Atcheson. It really is a fantastic book, but our family is especially drawn to Chapter 53, which is entitled, "Turned Down *Playboy* for His Youth Group." That section, of course, is about one Wesley Thomas Britt. It actually includes the story of how Wesley and I met—and how we came to be married. It relates Wesley's leadership through FCA and how he was a role model for his teammates. It details the events at which Wesley shared his faith to young people across Alabama, and how he glorified the Lord even during his most challenging times.

The chapter closes with these words:

"God made Wesley to be a big man, but his Christian faith is the biggest and strongest attribute he has. He's a giant for Jesus Christ."

God has given each of us amazing gifts. But he hasn't given us our gifts so that we can hoard them. His gifts are granted to us so that we can make other people's lives better. We each have a duty to show others the way to go. To whom much is given, much is required.

There have been people throughout my life who planted trees whose shade they knew they would never sit in.

Remember that no matter where you're standing, you're there as a result of *a lot of people* doing *a lot of things*. Yes, we have to handle what's in our control along the way. But people help us throughout the journey. If we can do that for somebody else, if we can be that person who empowers someone to do more, to be more, to give more—allowing them to be their best self—we have an obligation to do so. And I promise you, it's worth it. People are worth it.

CHAPTER 13

Work on Yourself at Work

MOST OF US WILL SPEND more than one-third of our lifespan at work, so a large portion of being our best selves comes down to how we handle being at our workplace. Getting this time right not only leads to increased job performance and career opportunities, but it can also result in a happier, more fulfilling life in general.

First, some good news: the lessons, values, and advice contained in the previous chapters very much apply to life at work. So, we're not reinventing the wheel here. Those things should act as the foundation on which you rely to address whatever particular situation life throws your way. We're not throwing the playbook out while we're on the job—we're simply applying it to the unique demands, expectations, and realities found in the modern workplace.

I have been fortunate to work in a multitude of places and for a variety of people. I've seen the good, the bad, and the ugly. From starting out at my own family's small businesses and other local small businesses in the Wiregrass when I was growing up to working in the US Senate, at a major flagship university, at two law firms, the US Senate again, and with businesses of all sizes and sectors at Alabama's business council, I've experienced a great deal.

In some areas, I was adequately prepared going into a workplace. However, there were plenty of times I needed to learn as I earned. Some of this happens through pure trial and error—and that's perfectly normal. Other lessons are gleaned from mentors and colleagues. No matter who you are or what you do for a living, there are things we all wish we had been taught earlier in life.

YOUR FIRST SIX MONTHS: YOUR BASELINE

In professional life, whether we like it or not, first impressions can make or break you. However, first impressions in the workplace are about more than a single moment or interaction.

For better or worse, your first six months at any job create the baseline by which you will be judged. This initial phase sets the tone for you and establishes how you are perceived by your peers—your workplace reputation, if you will. It determines what your manager comes to expect from you and, in many cases, what is possible for you.

It's vital to set a strong baseline. We all have bad days. We all have sleepless nights. And I can guarantee you that life will have its ups and downs. None of us can ever predict exactly what this rollercoaster will look like, but we know there will be peaks and valleys. It could be the unexpected twists and turns of a natural disaster or a family emergency. It could be an injury or health challenge. There will always be things along our journey that we can't fully anticipate or prepare for.

When these sudden curveballs are thrown our way, it's very

likely that we're going to operate below our baseline at work. A temporary dip in performance is natural while our time and attention are elsewhere. Now, anyone in a workplace facing a situation like this should be afforded grace. However, the reality is that we're likely to be shown more grace—and potentially for a longer time period—if we have set our standard at a high level. People know that our dip in performance is the exception, not the rule, because of the unassailably positive baseline we first established in that work environment.

The inverse situation is also true. If your first six months sets a weak baseline, even an increase in your job performance afterward will be unlikely to fully change people's negative perception of you in the workplace. They may doubt the uptick as a temporary surge and wonder how long it will last, believing that you will soon revert to the rule—which, in this case, is the lower bar you put in place for yourself.

Think about it this way. You can have two employees separately produce the exact same quality of work product. Employee A is someone who set a strong baseline in their first six months on the job. Now when Employee A's supervisor sees high-quality work from them, the reaction is something along the lines of, "Yeah, this is great. Just like I've come to expect. Employee A is dependable. I can always count on them." However, Employee B is someone who failed to set a strong standard for themselves. They are afflicted by low expectations. So, when their supervisor sees high-quality work from them now, the reaction is akin to, "That's weird. Their usual performance isn't this good."

Their quality of work was the same. But for Employee B, their new positive performance primarily reminded their supervisor of their traditional lower baseline. When that supervisor has to choose just one of them to assign an important task, they are going to pick Employee A every time.

So, how do you set a baseline like Employee A did? It goes back to doing the little things right and focusing on some key areas that you—and only you—can control.

1. Be on time.
2. Show up early and stay late when needed.
3. Complete the task and close the loop.
4. Have a positive attitude and find ways to improve.
5. Volunteer to help.
6. Go the extra mile.
7. Be intentional about how you present yourself.

Start with this checklist. Combine these simple items with consistently executing your assigned responsibilities and tasks, and you'll have a sound foundation and be well on the way to achieving professional success. You're not going to get everything perfectly right in your first six months, but displaying dependability will help you stand out among your peers and build the reputation you need to thrive long-term.

Potential References Are Everywhere

Don't forget that everyone is a potential reference, not just your boss. The standard you set from the start is what someone will remember as you move forward. Your first six months at one job could impact your ability to land the next one five years down the line, whether you're applying to a new workplace or you're vying for the big promotion. This is especially true in this digital age.

In days past, the three references on your résumé might be the only people with whom a potential employer would speak in the hiring process. Nowadays, they can look at your Facebook page for mutual friends or your LinkedIn profile for connections, and see whether they personally know anyone else to whom they could speak more candidly about your candidacy. They might reach out to a random former coworker you barely knew. Your baseline is pretty much all you have in that scenario. If your standards were set high, that person is likely to say something along the lines of, "I don't know them well, but they had a great reputation around the office." However, if your bar was low, that answer goes something like, "I remember they were always late." The last time you were late for work might have been four years ago. But if that was your initial reputation in a workplace, it can stick with you indefinitely.

So dig in early. This will raise your professional floor and ceiling in a lasting way.

BACK TO THE BASICS

Immediate first impressions are important, too. This shouldn't have to be said, but it needs to be. You'd be shocked by the percentage of people entering the workforce today who have never been taught the basics of professional etiquette and interpersonal behavior. And while times may have changed, these things will never go out of style.

Let's start with meeting someone for the first time. Make and maintain eye contact. Be present in the moment. Look at them, not through or past them. Speak with confidence and warmth—don't mumble—and say your name clearly. Give a firm handshake.

Smile. And listen—because you're going to have to remember their name and, depending on the exact interaction, potentially more.

Continue your intentionality of making eye contact, listening, and speaking clearly in the conference room setting as well. Look at the person who is speaking, engage, and take notes (on paper, not on your phone) if necessary. When you have the opportunity to speak, be conscious of the little things. Don't swivel back and forth in your chair as you make your remarks. No matter how knowledgeable you are on the subject matter, it gives the appearance of nervousness and can often be distracting. Try to eliminate your use of "umm," "like," and "ahh." And be concise. People tend to think that more is better, and that is simply not the case. Speak up, make your point, but don't consume more of the meeting time than necessary.

Athleisure Is for Running Errands, Not Board Rooms

Appearances matter when it comes to first impressions, as well. Present yourself how you want to be perceived. Dress not just for the job that you have, but the job you want. The value of good hygiene can't be overstated—hair, dental, nails, and—for the guys—facial hair. One note—your shoes are actually one of the first things people will notice. And do you know why? Because unconsciously in a new situation as we work to maintain comfort, we look down. Think about it. Unless your job requires work boots (in which case the dirtier, the better), keep your shoes clean and professional. For men—polishing your shoes the old-fashioned way goes a long way. For the ladies—while closed-toed shoes tend to be the safe bet, if open-toed shoes work in your professional environment *make sure* your toenails are painted. Which brings me to this—if a piece of clothing was designed to be worn at a gym or a yoga studio, it probably isn't right for the office. Look, I get it—those Lululemon pants probably cost more than a pantsuit, and no doubt they are more comfortable. But they're still not professional attire.

Put Your Phone Down

Another way to make a good impression and allow yourself to be more efficient and organized is to have a thoughtful process regarding the notes you take throughout the day. First, I think it comes off as incredibly rude when people are sitting in a meeting and "taking notes" on their phone. You end up looking at your phone instead of being engaged with the people around you. Worse, I have absolutely *no* idea if you are texting, commenting on a friend's social media post, returning emails, or *actually taking notes*. My immediate thought when someone pulls out their phone and starts typing is that if you have something better to do, I surely do, too. So, get off your phone and back to old school pen and paper.

On that note, I was the most productive when I kept all my notes in one place and consistently in the same type of notebook. Find a notebook that you really like and go ahead and stock up. This way, when you fill one up, you can write the dates covered on the outside of the notebook, grab an identical one, and continue the cycle. This allows for easy storage along with the best way to locate notes if you need them again. By a quick search of your calendar, you can find the meeting date and the corresponding notes. Another benefit is that you get conditioned to the process you create, the structure of the notebook, and as a result you become more productive. I am of the mindset that a variety of notebooks, pens, or office supplies is simply a distraction. Find what you like, and stock up on that.

Show People You Mean Business

Next, always have business cards on you. I've seen some great digital business card services used recently. I recommend that you download one so that you are prepared to take advantage of it supplementally. But there is still no substitute for putting the real thing in someone's hand. There is something about the weight and design of a good business card that says you, well, mean business. Also, if you really want to increase the odds that you end up in someone's contact list, help the recipient out and include your QR code for ease of entry.

Speaking of, be intentional when you receive someone else's. I know that I've been guilty in the past of telling myself I would get around to storing someone's contact information or that I would follow-up with them in a few days. But inevitably, we forget. We'll be cleaning out our purse, our briefcase, or our desk drawer in two months, and a stack of business cards will fall out.

To avoid this scenario, get into a habit of taking action at the end of the same day you receive someone's card. Input their information into your contacts along with a note with context about how and where you met them, as well as any other personally identifiable information your initial conversation entailed. This could include a reminder about the mutual acquaintance who introduced you or the fact that you know their roommate from college. Then, send them a brief email expressing that it was nice to meet them, along with any other relevant follow-up information.

First impressions are undoubtedly key. But so are second impressions—which is why the above is so critical. You don't want to get yourself into an awkward situation where you forget someone's name because you weren't really listening or weren't really present when they introduced themselves. You also don't want to forget a pivotal part of the opening conversation you had with someone. Imagine that you had an introductory business dinner with someone but then forget important details about their family or a major event in their life—that's the kind of thing that people remember when you can't put the pieces together next time that you see them. Listening is the least you can do for someone.

Lastly, follow through. If you left with an action item from the conversation, a quick and efficient follow-up is key to building a good baseline with that person. Jot a note down on their business card about the action item, and when you are inputting the contact that evening *or the next morning*, it will serve as an important reminder. It's a reality that we all struggle to remember things from time to time amid the busyness of life. So, set up a process that gets you off on the right foot with a future colleague, client, or reference.

Use Your Words

Speaking of impressions, it is important that you project confidence with your words—written or spoken. Younger professionals have a tendency to apologize for asking a question. They send an email that begins with "I am so sorry to bother you" or they ask a more seasoned employee a question that begins with "I *just* was wondering." There is a difference in being polite and giving your power away with your words. Younger women tend to especially struggle with this balance. They sometimes soften their phrasing by turning what should be a statement into a question. This is a mistake. Remember—you can be kind and direct at the same time. It's the most effective way to communicate.

And when you choose to write your words instead of speak them, go easy on the exclamation points! Exclamation points are rarely appropriate for professional communications. Use them sparingly and only to indicate excitement rather than emphasis or urgency. Think "Great job!" or "Congratulations!" rather than "The project deadline is in two days!" Also, get the emojis out of your professional communications. There may be an occasional occurrence where one is appropriate, but using them consistently in professional communication is an absolute *no go*. You might think it makes you look cool or approachable, but a string of emojis actually just makes you look juvenile and unprofessional.

Emojis in texts with your friends? One hundred percent go for it. Emails to your boss, clients, or customers? Probably not the best idea. Use. Your. Words.

Put It in the Mail

Finally, and this is a big one: invest in good stationery and habitually use it. The art of writing a good thank you note is dying right now. We all need to be more intentional about expressing our gratitude or acknowledging someone's good work, both in our personal lives and in professional settings. Whether it is a spoken word, a text, or an email, there is power in saying, "Thank you," or, "Job well done." It spreads good will for both the person expressing appreciation and the person on the receiving end. Just the sheer acknowledgment can transform someone's day and give them the motivation and encouragement to do more—to be their best.

While expressions of gratitude are meaningful in every form, there is still no substitute for a thank you note, handwritten in ink. People know that it takes time and intentionality to write, and it also shows maturity, organization, and class.

I've seen a number of people do this well throughout my life, but someone who really stands out for their mastery of the art is Jim Bayless. I met Jim when I was a young staffer in the Hart Senate Office Building in Washington, and he became an instant mentor. He set the perfect example of how a lasting impact can be made through a handwritten note. My parents still have the letter he sent them after my wedding. Eloquently and in the moment, he wrote about how much he and his wife, Liz, enjoyed the weekend and thanked them. And I'll never forget the letter Jim sent me after Liz and he attended my swearing-in ceremony. These intentional, authentic touches meant the world to my family and me.

I'd encourage young people currently in school to practice your handwriting—yes, we are moving continuously into a more digital age, but there is still a lot of value in being able to write (both in cursive and in print) beautifully. I'll admit—I wish I would've followed my own advice a few decades ago. "Beautiful" is not how I'd describe my handwriting. But whether you're like me or you've conquered calligraphy—it doesn't have to be long and it doesn't have to be perfect—just take the time to write that note.

One tip to turn this from a resolution to a reality—force yourself to actually take that time by carving out and guarding that time on a regular, scheduled basis. Whether it's weekly, bi-weekly, or monthly, hold a block of time on your calendar when you pen handwritten notes and do nothing else. We all get busy, and the note you'll get around to writing "soon" will end up not getting done if you don't institute a process to get it done. These can be thank you notes, and they can also be notes of congratulations, well-wishes, or sympathy. No matter the message you want to convey, it comes across more powerfully if you make and take the time to write it down and put it in the mail.

Emily Post Lives On

It might seem old-fashioned, but proper etiquette is still in style. This is especially important if you have the type of job that involves dining with clients or colleagues. Brush up on your decorum. It might seem obvious, but the little things matter. Know that you put your napkin in your lap before looking at the menu, which piece of silverware to use when, and that everyone should be served before you eat. And don't overserve yourself—your work outing *isn't* spring break.

Do all of this, and you'll nail initial impressions and be more memorable along the way.

WORKPLACES ARE ABOUT PEOPLE JUST AS MUCH AS THE WORK

Look, don't get me wrong—your job absolutely is about doing your job well. But being a part of a workplace comes down to much more than the work itself.

How you treat and function alongside the people in your workplace is a critical component of your career success—and your life. No matter how good you are at your job, if you are toxic in the workplace, you will not be there long.

The Golden Rule. Again.

First, don't forget that how you treat people matters. I want to work alongside people who treat the woman who cleans the restroom with the same respect they treat the principal or CEO. If you act like you're above anyone—or above any type of honest work—you'll end up setting yourself back at work and in life.

You'd be surprised by how some people treat individuals that they think cannot benefit them. A handful of months after being sworn into office, I walked into an event room in the Capitol for a meeting. The crowd was mostly comprised of people I'd never met—stakeholders representing various groups. There were a few minutes left before the meeting was scheduled to start, so I began to mingle and introduce myself to people standing around the room. There was a colleague from another state in front of me doing the same thing.

After meeting several perfectly friendly people, I reached one gentleman. I had just seen him warmly shake the other Senator's hand. So, I stuck out my hand, smiled, and said, "Hello." He looked at me, retracted his hand, and kept moving—completely leaving me hanging. I was more surprised than embarrassed or insulted, so I quickly moved on to the next person in the queue. They recognized me and said something along the lines of, "Good to see you, Senator."

After I finished that pleasant exchange, I turned around—and there was the gentleman who not even two minutes ago had snubbed me. I could tell he was mortified—he must have heard the other person call me, "Senator."

"I'm so sorry," he said. "I didn't realize *you* were a Senator."

I told him I accepted his apology, smiled, and got on with my day. Mistakes happen. And the truth is that this has happened to me more times than I can count. I choose to forgive and move on. But there is a lesson here we can all learn from: I shouldn't be treated differently because I'm a Senator. And we shouldn't treat others with different levels of respect or kindness because of how "important" you perceive them to be.

Always default to kindness, respect, and integrity. Practice the Golden Rule at all times.

And when you find yourself in a challenging situation, it is usually best to take a deep breath and a step back. Collect your thoughts, give yourself time to process, and be intentional before hitting send on your response. You cannot take your words—or email—back. Remember, everything comes full circle. Your intern one day could be your boss the next. Your band director could be your mayor. Your student could be your US Senator.

Hunger Games Was Meant for Entertainment, Not Imitation

Healthy relationships at work are built on trust and respect. Your workplace shouldn't be a Hunger Games environment. If that's the kind of culture that is celebrated at your jobsite, don't participate in it—and get out of there as soon as you can. You should be surrounded by teammates, not opponents. And unfortunately, as hard as you try to separate the two, the toxicity at work spills into life at home.

To do your part to foster a team mentality, you have to be a team player. It's not hard to figure out if someone is there because they believe in the mission or if they're there to serve themselves. If they are there for themselves, it may take some time, but they eventually end up on an island with no way off. So, have your teammates' backs—don't be the person your coworkers suspect will stab them in the back the second it suits their own individual goals.

Be the kind of person who takes the blame but spreads the credit. Acknowledge and celebrate others' successes. Choose and embrace team-first selflessness. Release negativity. Remind yourself that "it's a great day to be alive," and listen to the song—or whatever song works for you—if you need it. Then, bring that positivity into the workplace and spread it.

Philippians 4:8 is one of my favorite pieces of scripture:

Whatever is true, whatever is noble, whatever is right, whatever is pure, whatever is lovely, whatever is admirable—if anything is excellent or praiseworthy—think about such things.

When we keep our minds on inherently positive things, when our focus is unwavering and our direction is firm, our thoughts will precede the type of actions we desire.

On that note... Don't be about the drama. Be about the work. And be a good colleague. Keep the main thing the main thing.

Water cooler gossip—whether it's actually done in the office or if it's over text nowadays—never ends well. Those little moments in the breakroom between coworkers should be reserved for asking them how their kid's soccer game was, not badmouthing or spreading rumors about another colleague. Don't be the kind of person in a workplace instigating trouble. Because no matter how good your work is, your drama isn't worth it.

It's inescapable that workplaces will have interpersonal drama and interoffice politics to some degree. But do your best to stay above the fray. If people start to engage in gossip or pour fuel on the fire, walk away. You don't have to be a part of the problem just because others around you are. Nothing good is going to come out of that kind of behavior and it becomes toxic. And remember: what goes around, comes around. That's a fact.

Set a New Standard

You will inevitably have to deal with challenging coworkers and supervisors. I've had my share of them—I saw everything from those who would always pit colleagues against each other to those who refused to take any blame, letting their own insecurities strangle the potential of those around them and making you feel like you had to sleep with one eye open at all times. There is a temptation to bottle up their bad behaviors and toxicity and eventually pass it on to others when you have the "opportunity" by making others go through the same things you had to go through. I implore you *not* to do this. Instead, take those moments as opportunities to treat others the way you wish you had been treated. Take note of how they mishandled a situation and learn from it. Then do better and be better by *not* repeating their mistake. Set a new example—a standard—for others to follow.

This is the hallmark of a real leader in the workplace. You don't have to be a supervisor to be a leader—and being a supervisor doesn't make you a leader. Act like a leader, and I promise you, it will not go unnoticed.

Don't Be a Schmoozer

We all know that person—the guy or gal who spends most of their time at work schmoozing instead of working. It could be kissing up to the boss or constantly yakking it up in an attempt to curry favor with others. People see right through that. When you get into the habit of schmoozing, people will come to view you as a phony. They won't be able to trust you're being authentic in interactions, because people think you are constantly performing in order to serve your own interests. Don't become that person. Be a workhorse, not a show horse.

OWN YOUR SPACE

While other people are key pieces to the puzzle in your workplace, *you*—and only you—are ultimately responsible for doing your job and doing it to the best of your ability.

Your job is your space, so own it.

Actually Read It

That being said—actually do your own work. That means proofreading your own material (getting help or a second set of eyes is fine, but you still need to own the end product). We get caught up in the world of getting it done fast instead of getting it done right. You'd be amazed by the number of times someone presented me with "their" work product, but they proceed to look puzzled when

I hand it back to them with glaring typos or inaccuracies circled. They would've caught those things if they had simply read what they were about to give me.

The One Page You Can't Get Wrong

The same thing goes for your résumé. Proofread it. Please, I'm begging you. A lot of people (including me) will immediately throw out any résumé with a typo. If you cannot take the time and attention to get just one page right, how can someone trust you with the responsibilities of a job?

Understand the Assignment

Knowing what you're supposed to do is the bare minimum. To reach the next level, know why you're doing something. At work, this means understanding the purpose of each assignment. This will allow you to complete the assignment at a higher level. For example, if you are preparing a written memo for your boss, ask yourself how they are actually going to use that information—and then think about how you can format your material to make their life easier.

Knowing the purpose of a task will also enable you to think down the road to next steps. That assignment is likely part of a larger project or end goal. If you know the bigger picture, you can contribute in a more meaningful way to the team.

Excuses Get Old Quick

Failure in the workplace, as in life, is not a matter of *if*, but *when*. So, when it happens, what separates the best from the rest is how you react. Don't make excuses. Engage in honest self-evaluation to analyze how you got there. What was under your control that should be corrected to avoid a repeat result in the future? The best thing you can do is take accountability and acknowledge your mistakes. Proactively own up to the error before you have to and know the takeaways. Explain how you are fixing the situation and how you will ensure it doesn't happen again.

You need to mean this too. You can't just say that it won't happen again—you have to actually take the necessary corrective action. A primary frustration for supervisors is having to correct the same thing over and over again.

Hot Wash It

This is another area in which having a process and executing that process is integral to success. You should be in the habit of regimented self-evaluation, regardless of whether an outcome is viewed as a success or failure. There are always things that can be done better, that can be improved on, or that can be added to.

Immediately after a project, event, presentation, or any other milestone at work, candidly assess what worked and what didn't work—in other words, hot wash it. This is a term that comes from the old practice of soldiers after they fired their weapons. The weapons were doused in extremely hot water to remove grit and residue. This quick, no fuss cleaning can save a lot of time and headache later.

Evaluate what could have been improved or done differently and if there is anything else that should be tweaked the next time around. It is also important to note what went well or what worked. It helps to undergo this process right away, when it is fresh in your head. You may tell yourself you'll remember a month from now, but the reality is that details—the very details that need scrutiny—are tough to remember after the moment has passed.

This is something I implemented when I was president and CEO of Alabama's business council. After every event, we would undergo a self-evaluation of what went wrong, what went right, and what could be added the next time. Create a checklist and continue to refine it. We scrutinized the smallest details, like if there should have been four check-in tables instead of three. But we also studied the bigger ticket items, like if the on-stage programming ran too long or the A/V production could have used improvement. All of it matters.

Feedback Helps Prevent Future Failures

Not all evaluation will be self-generated in the workplace, of course. The way you accept and handle feedback—including constructive criticism—is important. People tend to have a natural instinct of self-preservation that defensively manifests itself as deflection and blame-shifting when confronted about a mistake. But this is exactly the opposite reaction we should have. Number one, this kind of response is self-destructive because it is ultimately an impediment to bettering ourselves and achieving success moving forward. Additionally, other people will start to not trust you (as well as not respect you professionally) if you become known as someone who continually makes excuses instead of owning missteps and making corrections.

You should also openly welcome and embrace feedback. Now, don't be that person hovering over your supervisor twice a day asking if there is something you can do better. However, you should be intentional early in a job to directly and confidently say that you welcome comments on how you can improve or do things differently any time your supervisor sees something. "Please don't hesitate to let me know if there is ever something I can do better. I'm always looking for ways to improve and would appreciate any feedback you can give me. My feelings won't be hurt." This way, *when* there is something that the supervisor notices, it is likely they will bring it to you constructively rather than letting it fester.

This type of open and direct communication—in which you're fostering a climate of conversation rather than confrontation—is integral to achieving professional success. Apply the same line of thought to when you feel strongly about something. Whether it is advocating for a point of view or a strategy or disagreeing with someone else's, don't be afraid to push back. Again, you can be direct and respectful at the same time.

Speaking Too Often Is Often Too Much

Speaking up is important. But don't be the boy who cried wolf. If you're going to speak out, actually have something to say. Everyone quickly grows tired of those people who talk in meetings—or on a conference call—just to hear themselves talk. Those are the people others tune out. So, when you eventually do have an important point or argument to make, no one is actually listening. You've lost before you can even make your case. Sometimes saying nothing at all accomplishes the most.

Look for Opportunities to Earn It, Then Own It

Undoubtedly, there is a time and a place for just about everything. Picking your battles and choosing your openings is the name of the game. There is a balancing act between humility and confidence that is constant in the workplace.

That being said, very little in professional life will come with an embossed invitation. There won't be a flashing neon sign that tells you it's time. Seize opportunities by saying "yes" to assignments, and then use them to show people what you are made of. Work hard and earn people's respect. Once you have earned it, pull your seat up at the table. You are not entitled to a seat; you are entitled to an opportunity to prove that you belong there. You'll know in your gut when that time has arrived. Trust yourself when that happens.

LITERALLY, OWN YOUR SPACE

A big part of workplace success is your actual workspace. Keep yours tidy—people project a messy desk as a disorganized and out of control employee.

One of my favorite tips here—keep a plant on your desk (or in your office). It makes you feel at home, and it can brighten not just your day but the day of everyone who sees it. I am rather serious about following this myself. After I was elected to the Senate, I bought a couple of plants from Vinson Market, a local small business in Montgomery, for my new office. I then carried the plants, each in paper bags, with me on my flight up to DC. Getting those plants through airport security didn't make me too popular with a TSA agent or two, but the end result was well worth it.

Don't Stink up the Place

Some more seemingly obvious dos and don'ts pertain to your workspace as well.

If you use the fridge, don't leave things in there to expire. If you use the kitchen or another shared space, clean up after yourself (including the microwave). And don't be that person who brings smelly food into the office.

Speaking of smelly, definitely make sure you keep your breath in check—but choose mints over gum. The bottom line is that your boss sees you chewing gum, and I assure you, they think it's unprofessional. The same goes for clients or customers. Someone trying to talk with gum in their mouth appears disrespectful. No one needs to see the neon green glob roaming around the inside of your mouth while you're trying to make a pitch. The truth is that we cannot concentrate on what you are saying, because we are too busy trying to figure out when that thing is going to swan-dive right out onto the conference table. And, regardless of how subtle you think you're being, you are still making some smacking noises when chewing—and your coworkers don't like it, whether anyone says anything or not.

Remember, Your Posts Are Public

Finally, when it comes to your workspace in modern times, the digital space is fair game too. That means your personal life is your personal life—until you publish it online. And don't try the "my account is private" response to make yourself feel better about your cyber conduct. You know what a screenshot is, so keep that excuse moving.

If you want it to be private, actually keep it private. In a 21st-century, global economy, the lines of demarcation between private and professional realms are much more blurred than they were even 15 years ago. Oversharing on social media can now cost you more than friends—it can damage your career prospects. So, think twice before you post, comment, or retweet. If you wouldn't say it to someone's face in person, is it something you should be saying in cyberspace? We should not have separate value sets for how we behave online versus offline. Don't lose sight of being your best, even when you're behind a username or avatar.

Remote Work Has Rules Too

Like it or not, remote and hybrid work arrangements are here to stay. However, it's important to realize that you can't just throw out the rulebook when you're not working at a physical worksite. The principles found throughout the rest of this chapter still very much apply to working away from an office building. If anything, you have to be more intentional to succeed and stand out positively while working remotely.

For example, you need to be savvy about communicating with your boss and building relationships with your colleagues. You don't have the opportunity to catch up with your boss in the hallway or bond with coworkers around the water cooler. Instead, you have to proactively check in with your boss and create opportunities to connect with those whom you work with. There is no doubt that remote work can be isolating for people, so carve out time to establish those fibers of connectivity that would typically form in a traditional workplace.

While some aspects are different in remote working, others remain roughly the same. When in a Zoom meeting, for instance, the standards of your physical space and how you conduct yourself should not change. Your appearance and behavior should be professional. *Yes*, you need to turn the camera on. Your background should be clean and organized, just like a desk space or office.

Remember, a cluttered space signals a cluttered mind. Don't forget to mute yourself when you're not talking. And look—and actually *be*—engaged. Look into the camera—not off into the distance. The ground rules of being in a meeting don't get tossed out the window just because you're not in a conference room.

PROCESSES ARE PROTECTION

Put processes in place and be diligent in practicing them at the workplace. This will improve your job performance while also helping keep you from making mistakes.

I learned a tremendous amount about how to be meticulously process-oriented from one of my mentors, Anne Caldwell. One of the greatest lessons in this area was how to properly close the loop.

The Art of Closing the Loop

When someone at work, let's say your boss, assigns you a task, the ball is in your court until you *complete* (not just start) the task and then volley it back. Your first steps should include establishing a realistic timeline—one that you can stick to and ultimately do stick to—and setting that expectation with your boss. If they need it done sooner than you propose, this gives them the ability to tell you on the front-end. You also want to lay out other relevant details, so they know what to expect of your work. This is another opportunity for them to ensure you're on the same page—they can redirect, clarify, or adjust as needed before you get too far down the road. This kind of predictability on both expectations and execution facilitates good results.

For example, your boss assigns you a legal brief. In turn, you advise that your plan is to deliver it to them on Thursday, focusing on A, B, C, and D. They might say that works perfectly. Or, they could let you know that they go before the judge on Thursday morning, so they need the brief on Wednesday. Maybe Thursday works, but they tell you, "Don't forget about X, Y, and Z when you're writing it." Either way, you're now on the same page and can proceed to execute the gameplan. Closing the loop happens when the project is completed and you directly let your boss know that it has been completed.

However, seemingly smaller—simpler—tasks can actually be trickier when it comes to closing the loop. Consider this situation: your boss asks you to find out from Client A about detail X.

So, you call Client A. You get their voicemail and leave one asking for a return call. Now, here comes the part where a lot of people get it wrong.

You need to do two more things. First, immediately send Client A an email saying you just left them a voicemail and you look forward to connecting (soon, at their convenience, or at their earliest convenience, depending on the urgency of your task). Second, if you haven't heard back in 24 hours (you can wait a little longer if you have a more extended turnaround time), you should attempt to make contact again. If you are unsuccessful a second time, be sure to follow up with your boss to let them know of your effort. You don't need to do this in a way that is intrusive to your boss's schedule—shoot them a quick email, text, or even slip them a note to provide this quick update. Many times, your boss may have an additional avenue through which Client A can be contacted or may want you to start pursuing a different route.

When you do these two things, your boss knows that you're on top of the task and has the opportunity to redirect if necessary. This is an important step. However, remember that the loop is only officially closed when you have communicated back not just that the task has been attempted, but that the task is actually complete.

If you instead had just left a voicemail and hoped to get a return call, you would have left yourself exposed. Consider the situation where Client A doesn't return the call. In a few days, your boss asks you for detail X. You don't have it still. You tell them you haven't heard from Client A. In this scenario, your boss is left to wonder if you even reached out at all. Even if you did, did you follow-up? Your boss isn't inspired with confidence that you're on top of the task or may be frustrated because they would have given you alternative instructions if they knew you were having trouble. Ultimately, they question their ability to depend on you the next time a similar task arises.

The most important fact of this lesson is that if your boss has to ask you if a task you have been assigned has been completed (or for an update), you have already *failed*. Dependability is a rare find. If you earn the reputation of being dependable, you can essentially make yourself indispensable in the workplace.

Create and Keep Receipts

Another key workplace process is to create and keep receipts—and, no, and I don't mean the kind you get at CVS. It is smart to keep a written record you can fall back on if you need to back up or confirm something you did. Most of this record you may never intend to use again. But it will be the one time you don't keep a record of something when you end up needing it the most.

In the previous example, your receipt was that follow-up email you sent Client A. If Client A never gets back to you but runs into your boss in a couple of weeks, your boss might inquire directly for an answer. "Did so-and-so call you about this?" Client A, potentially embarrassed or defensive from not returning the call, might revert to pretending they never got a call—or a voicemail. But, if you have it in writing, you have protected yourself.

Receipts are also useful in hedging against the inevitability of memory lapses. There might be a project you essentially need to replicate two years down the line, but you can't remember exactly what you did, how you did it, or who you talked to the first time around. If you kept good receipts, you have a playbook waiting in the wings—saving yourself time and increasing efficiency. And, if you did a self-evaluation after the initial project like I previously touched on, you'll be ready not just to replicate it but to improve upon it.

YOUR TIME IS YOUR GREATEST GIFT—USE IT WISELY

The most valuable resource you have in life—and in the workplace—is time. Correctly managing how you utilize your time may just be the most important thing you can do.

We live in a time of short attention spans. 24/7 cable news. Social media blurbs. Memes. Now, shorter and shorter social media videos. We are constantly being pulled to move on to the next thing—and quickly. But there is a big difference between being fast and being efficient.

Multitasking Is Often Asking for Trouble

One of the things I see people, especially younger people entering professional life, get wrong is the inclination to multitask for the sake of multitasking. The thought is something along the lines of, "If we can do more at once, we can do more overall." Or, sometimes they just like the appearance of being busy and juggling multiple balls at the same time. Yet, this can backfire—the line of thought can end up being flat-out wrong, and all of the balls can come crashing down to the ground.

Don't be afraid to monotask. Doing one thing at a time—and doing that thing efficiently and well—is tried-and-true for a reason. Giving tasks your undivided attention and efforts, just like people, is often the best course of action.

My advice to achieving this is to create to-do lists and churn through them one-by-one. I find that it frequently helps to start with small, more straightforward tasks and then work your way up to the bigger, more complex ones. This builds your mental momentum and gives you a sense of accomplishment and renewed energy as you continue working through your list of tasks.

Make Big Projects Small

In life, some goals are so big that they seem unattainable. When that is the case, many times we don't know where to start. So, we just don't. What I have found over time to be the most effective in working toward that big goal is setting smaller ones that—while still requiring hard work—seem clearly achievable. They help me hone my skills, make progress, and show discipline toward the larger goal, and the completion of each objective gives me the confidence to achieve more. By mastering the little things, you build up to the big ones. The same thing applies at work.

In order to get big projects, assignments, or tasks effectively executed, sometimes it's best to break them up. Work backward from the goal to create the timeline needed. Once you have that, you can then divide up the goals. You will be able to keep yourself on task and on time. This can also help you develop a better work product in the end.

Be a Sponge

Something I did not do well earlier in my career was actually absorbing the information at my fingertips. I became too focused on checking task items off of my list and started to operate on autopilot. I was robotically getting tasks done—and done well—but I wasn't taking in the information or intricacies involved in the assignment. I was especially guilty of this during my first months working in Senator Shelby's communications office. That was a big mistake. In a press role like that, pretty much everything that touches the office came across my desk, from news of the day to committee hearing preparation and legislative text.

I finally realized that the only person keeping me from learning and doing more was *me*. I was causing my own personal and professional growth to plateau by not being a sponge and truly taking in the expertise and information around me. Instead of merely focusing on what I needed to know to draft a press release or complete another narrow task, I began to take pride in really learning the ins and outs of the many subjects to which I was being exposed.

Seizing the knowledge at my fingertips as I continued to complete tasks and do my job was a game changer for my professional growth and career trajectory.

You can gain skills and expertise from the people around you as well as the resources available to you. Always be in a constant state of learning. Take the time to read what comes across your desk and email. And don't just read to check a box—read for comprehension. There is significant power and value in being the most informed person in a workplace—or in any room.

Timing Is Everything

Speaking of rooms (and this is one of those things that should be common sense but isn't very commonly followed), being on time doesn't just mean that you shouldn't be late for work. It means that you should arrive promptly for meetings, events, lunches, and scheduled happenings of any sort. This is courteous and professional. And remember that when you show up or start a meeting late, it sends the message to others that you don't value their time. Those who have worked with me before will tell you that if you want to be on time, be five minutes early.

The scheduled time is the start time, not the arrival time. You should be prepared to begin at the time on the calendar—slides ready, notebook out, glasses on, coffee in the cup. If you show up exactly when scheduled, you're effectively late. That kind of thinking also gives you a little cushion for the inevitable delay while you're en route—whether it's traffic on the road or a packed elevator in your own office building. Bottom-line: meetings, calls, and events should *start* on time.

Just Deal with It

Time gets away from us all. Before we know it, another day, week, month, or year has gone by. This is why we need to be intentional about addressing things in the moment. If we let time pass, the thing we meant to do will get swept away with its passage.

To help avoid being time's victim in the workplace, try to respond to things when they are open. I'm talking about emails and text messages especially. It can also be a voicemail or a note left on your desk. And I'll admit—on many days I am actually *the worst* at following this advice. When it is in front of you, deal with it—or at least put it on your to-do list. If you tell yourself that you'll respond to someone later or come back around to a task without making a plan to actually execute, you'll likely forget to do it. Time will pass, and that thing won't get done—or that person will accidentally get ghosted.

Burning the Midnight Oil Isn't Always a Good Look

Finally, when the normal business day doesn't allow for enough time to get the job done, you are inevitably going to have to work late, work early, work weekends, or all of the above to get the job done. Your willingness to put in the work—even outside of normal business hours—is a positive thing in the workplace. Plain and simple: you have to be willing to do what it takes to get the job done.

However, you shouldn't drive yourself into the ground just to make it look like you're a hard worker. There should be a reason you're staying late or coming in early—and it shouldn't be an all-the-time kind of thing. You must create a work-life balance that is sustainable. Consistently working around the clock will inevitably lead to burnout and a work product that lacks the crispness you desire.

That being said, if you are a supervisor, don't email, text, or call at all hours of the night, on the weekends, or on holidays. The same goes for employees. It doesn't make you look like a workhorse when you consistently send emails at 2:00 am; it makes you look unhealthy and that you struggle in managing your time. It sends a sort of bizarre signal to those you work with and sometimes makes others feel like they are never *not* on-call.

Now, I get that things happen—I've certainly been there. So, if you are catching up on work or correspondence late at night, schedule that email to go out first thing in the morning, say at 6:04 am. And instead of texting colleagues questions at that hour, create a note on your phone—it could even be a shared one if it is someone you communicate with consistently—where you can list out the things to which you need answers. This allows you to keep the ball moving while also respecting their time at home, which is critically important. If you have a big event, meeting, or hearing, that is one thing, but otherwise wait until one hour before the normal workday is set to begin to start sending out those texts.

Creating this standard is important for two reasons: first, you are setting healthy boundaries for everyone involved, and second, when you call, email, or text at a traditionally unexpected time, they will know that you really need them and will answer immediately.

TAKE CARE OF YOURSELF

I know I just stressed the value and importance of time, which was true. But without *you* in the equation, time isn't doing you very much good.

We are not robots. While we have all seen workplaces that wished that were so, it isn't. We are complex people, all made in God's image, each with real needs, unique dreams, and nuanced preferences. And it is our own responsibility to take care of ourselves.

This means our physical health, our mental health, and our spiritual well-being. All three are vital. Not only can we not be our best at work if we don't take care of ourselves, but we'll find it impossible to live our purpose, as well.

Faith and Family First

A few pointers in this space—first, the demands of work and home can eat up the hours in our day before we know it. That is why you have to ensure that the things that are most important to your well-being don't get squeezed out. Grab your bible, find a devotional that you like, and set aside time for just you and the Lord. The stressors of the day can easily steal that time if we are not intentional about carving it out. Spending time with the Lord is absolutely the most important thing you will do each day.

Next, guard your family time. First, you must prioritize quality time with your spouse. There is a reason they tell you to never stop dating. It is important to realize that your dates don't have to be conventional. You know what your relationship needs more than others do. One of the things you need, whether you realize it or not, is to answer your spouse's phone calls. Silencing them sends the wrong message. If you absolutely have to hit ignore, make sure you send a quick text—and don't forget to follow up. There is something to be said for being worthy of a simple "hello."

Next, you don't get time back with your children, so know that every stage of your child's life is important. Being able to be present sometimes means having to pass on a work opportunity or having to work overtime to get the job done so that your child's activity is not what you cut when you are in a pinch.

Family and friends are important. And so is quality time with them. Whether it is a graduation, engagement party, or just an opportunity to be together, do your best to make it work. It might take some juggling, some sacrifices, and some creativity, but always remember what your priorities in life are and make sure others know your priorities as well. Don't let work consume you to the point where you forget to show up for the ones you love.

No One Wants Your Germs

In addition to getting your priorities in order, make sure you take care of yourself—and those around you. I think the pandemic made people more aware of this, but when you are sick, please stay home. I didn't get this *at all* when I first got into the workforce. I thought that by staying home I was somehow weak and that I would appear uncommitted to the team. However, I then had someone with small children tell me, "Please stay home when you don't feel well. None of us want to take what you have home with us." What I didn't realize until that moment was how rude (and selfish, ultimately) it is to come to work sick.

Get Moving

Make sure that in the busyness of the day that you take time for your physical health. Whether it is before work, during lunch, or on your way home, you need to move—at least a little. In addition to the obvious physical benefits of exercise, there is a direct link to your mental health, as well. Studies show that people who exercise regularly have better mental health and emotional well-being.

The common response I get when I suggest making just 20 minutes of physical exercise part of your daily routine is that there isn't enough time in the day. Do me a favor. Count up the minutes you scroll on various social media platforms every day and you will see that you actually have time to get in a longer walk or workout than you realize. You may have to adjust your schedule a little bit or *scroll a little less*, but I can promise you that you will feel better and perform better as a result.

Take a REAL Vacation

That brings me to this—actually be on vacation when you take vacation days. I'm not saying you have to actually travel somewhere, but you do need to check out from work. News flash: working remotely is not the same as taking time off. Look, we all need to recharge at times, but in order to do that, you have to truly unplug. Taking the time to do this is a sign of strength, not weakness.

In order to make your vacation a *real* vacation, be prepared. One: make sure you properly document the request and approval of your time off—meaning if there is no formal process, make sure to create your own receipt. Two: two weeks out, remind your supervisor and anyone with whom you might be working on a project that you will be out. Three: close the loop on any outstanding tasks or provide an update prior to being gone. Four: if there are outstanding obligations, reminders, or things that need to be taken care of when you are gone, think ahead and make sure those are covered. Five: don't forget to establish a proper auto-email response and phone message to point people in the right direction. Six: enjoy yourself.

Stepping Away Fosters More Productivity

Now, when you are at work—I have one central piece of advice to help you recharge during the day: Don't eat at your desk. Ok, I get you might have to have lunch at your desk on the occasional super-busy workday. But whenever humanly possible, don't do it. Get away to create a little mental break for yourself. Get some fresh air. Eat outside on a park bench. Eat in the courtyard. Eat with colleagues around a breakroom table or in a conference room. Meet someone for lunch. Wherever it is, try to create that space and that peace within your day.

Real-Time Résumé

One final tip for when you're at your desk—and this is another way to take care of yourself professionally: Keep a living copy of your résumé on your computer's desktop and constantly update it. Do this for two main reasons. One: you never know when you will need it, but many times it is when you least expect it. Two: you can more easily describe new skills or participation in projects in real-time rather than trying to remember them later down the line when you're wracking your brain about stuff to beef up your résumé.

This is something I instituted as Senator Shelby's chief of staff. Every year during the Senate's August state work period, I would make the entire office turn in an updated résumé to me as an accountability measure to ensure they were actually keeping up with it.

I recommend keeping a running list of everything (this is a much longer version of your résumé than you'll ever send out). When it does come time to apply for a new job, a civic or philanthropic position, or for a promotion, that's when you can cut this version down and tailor it to the opportunity for which you are applying. For example, your résumé for a leadership position in a community organization should likely look different than your résumé for a career-related move.

Hopefully some of this helps. But the most important thing is to figure out what works for you. There is no doubt that by taking care of yourself, you will be in the best position to succeed.

CHAPTER 14

Passing It On...

THERE IS NO GREATER JOY—and no greater responsibility—in life than helping raise the next generation. It's incredibly rewarding, and it's also challenging at the same time.

I speak from experience. My most fulfilling title in life is "Momma," and my most important job is being Bennett and Ridgeway's mom. Although, I am actually getting called just plain "Mom" these days, and that's a hard transition for me.

Everyone's path to parenthood is different. It's often messy—and majestic at the same time. It might not be exactly how we would have drawn it up or how we foresaw it. But it's all part of God's plan.

For Wesley and me, our road to being parents certainly wasn't a simple one. However, God was sending us signs along the way—whether we realized it in the moment or not.

This is a story that starts at Bama Bound. It was my very first day on campus in Tuscaloosa early during the summer of 2000. I was there for freshman orientation—and let's not forget, my mom had sent me by myself.

I was pretty nervous at the time—there was a lot to learn and a lot to take in. I drove over to the student center and checked in, before taking a seat in the student theater for the orientation programming. That's how I met Wesley Britt.

After I took my seat, I heard someone say my name. I turned and was glad to see a familiar face. It was Matthew Sanders, an incoming football player I knew. He said hello—and introduced me to his friend, Wesley. At six-foot-eight, he was pretty hard to miss. We talked a little bit before orientation began, and then we parted ways—at least for the moment.

The last orientation item that day was registration for classes. Student athletes and Honors program students got to register first, which meant we got to leave the student center around the same time. I was starting to walk out to my car when a rather huge stranger stopped me and asked if he and a friend could hitch a ride. He introduced himself as Justin Smiley. Although I had already deduced as much, he explained that he was on the football team. He said that one of his teammates was finishing up with registration and should be done any second, and he asked if I was willing to drive them back to the dorm. Before I knew it, there was Wesley again. Justin didn't know we had already met, so he made a show of introducing me to his friend, "Wes." He even started to go through all of Wesley's top high school football accolades and recruiting rankings.

Somehow, we ended up fitting three offensive linemen in my Firebird—Wesley, Justin, and Evan Mathis. Wesley sat up front. Years later, I found out that he didn't actually need a ride that day. He had his own truck at the student center the whole time.

I also eventually found out that he kept the little piece of paper on which I wrote my name and pager number for him. I know that

I'm dating myself here, but those were the days when someone had to page you so you could then find a landline from which to call them. The years have flown by and times have certainly changed, but I now have that piece of paper framed at our house.

So that was our meet-cute, but Wesley and I didn't have the most straightforward courtship. After that initial meeting, I walked into my very first class as a student at the University of Alabama, and there was Wesley. We quickly became best friends—we even went to lunch with each other every Friday during our four undergraduate years on campus. But we never dated in college, despite the multitude of signs God sent our way.

We actually were friends for nearly seven years before we went on our first date.

It was late January in 2007. I was working as Senator Shelby's press secretary at the time, and I had traveled from Washington to Alabama to staff the senator for some state events on his schedule. Wesley was playing for the Patriots but was back home for the start of the NFL off-season, following a loss to the Colts in the AFC Championship Game. I told Wesley I was going to visit my cousin, Parker McQueen, at Children's Hospital in Birmingham after I was done working. Wesley, of course, while in college had become close with my Uncle Mike and Parker had become special to Wesley, too. So, he came to pick me up so that we could head to the hospital together to visit Parker.

While we were at the hospital, Uncle Mike asked Wesley, "Well, where are you taking Katie for her birthday dinner next weekend?" I had almost forgotten my birthday was coming up. I didn't have any plans whatsoever. "I am sure she will be back in Washington," Wesley responded to him. I told him, "Actually, I'll be in Huntsville for work." So, Wesley took Uncle Mike's suggestion and brought me to Ruth's Chris in Huntsville on February 2. It was our first date after being best friends for six-and-a-half years.

The rest was history. We were married 13 months later, March 8, 2008, in Enterprise.

The person you should want to spend your life with needs to make you a better version of yourself. That person should be a true partner. And that's exactly what I have in Wesley. We certainly have had our fair share of struggles. Marriage is hard and is something you have to work on every day. But no doubt it is worth it. What an incredible blessing from God it is to be able to navigate life's ups and downs with my soulmate and best friend.

With Wesley playing for New England when we got married, I moved to Foxboro to begin our life together.

The Lord soon blessed us with a gift even more unimaginable—one that is equal parts sacred, beautiful, and fragile.

I was reminded of this fact in April 2009. Nearly nine months pregnant with Bennett, I got quite the scare.

It was already a time when I was flooded with all kinds of emotions. There was the expected excitement, nerves, and fear associated with being a first-time parent. Additionally, I had been told that because of Bennett's positioning and what they believed to be her size, I wasn't going to be able to have her naturally. I was sad and anxious about that news, and I felt like I was already falling short as a mother. But at the same time, above anything in the world, I wanted her to be safely delivered. My heart and my head were having a tug-of-war, and I was just along for the ride.

My doctor scheduled a C-section, and we started getting

everything in order. Many of our family members on both sides made their arrangements to come up to Massachusetts to be there for the big day.

That's when it happened—two days before I was set to arrive at the hospital to have Bennett.

I was at our two-story rental house. Wesley wasn't home at the time. And for some reason, at 39 weeks' pregnant, there I was running up the stairs. I shouldn't have been trying to move swiftly *anywhere*, much less up a flight of stairs.

I slipped and fell, landing directly and forcefully on the 90-degree angle of a stair—right on the precious place in my body where I was carrying my almost full-term daughter. I immediately screamed with every ounce of my soul, terrified that I might have just irreparably harmed my unborn child.

I flipped over and immediately began feeling for movement. *Please, please, please, PLEASE.* No matter what I tried, I couldn't get her to move. I couldn't get my sweet baby girl to move. Praying, I began to slide down the stairs, slowly, one-by-one, until I got to the landing at the bottom. I went and found my phone and called for help.

We loved living near the stadium in Foxboro, a relatively rural area. However, a downside of the location was my doctor being about 30 miles away—with traffic, easily a 45-minute drive—at Brigham and Women's Hospital in Boston.

I called my doctor and managed to explain what happened. They told me that I better come in to get checked out. *She isn't moving*, kept racing through my mind. Wesley quickly came home, got me into the truck, and we headed to Boston.

That felt like the longest car ride of my life. She still wouldn't move. When we got to the hospital, the agony of waiting and not knowing just grew worse. There were a few emergency situations ahead of me, so I had to sit in the waiting room for what seemed like an eternity. I prayed and prayed until my name was called.

When they got me into a room, they hooked me up and started listening for a heartbeat. I thanked God—after a few long seconds, they found one. Everything seemed fine, they said. A wave of relief washed over me, and after a few hours of precautionary observation, I was released to head home before returning for the scheduled delivery.

Bennett would arrive around lunchtime a couple of days later, weighing 7 pounds and 5 ounces. Less than 12 months later, she would get a baby brother when Ridgeway was born at 7 pounds and 13 ounces. And like so many pregnancies, there were challenging times along the way. At my very first doctor's appointment, they could not find Ridgeway's heartbeat. The moment they worked up the courage to tell me, my own heart stopped. I was sent home for five days—for what felt like an eternity. The tears and terrifying realization that I may have lost my child brought me to my knees. I prayed for the opportunity to raise him. Five days later, I received an answer to that very prayer when the sound of a heartbeat came through loud and clear.

Parenthood is not a destination, it's a journey. Wesley and I are still learning as we go. We don't get it right all the time—and no one does. That's totally normal, because perfect doesn't exist in parenting.

We certainly don't know it all and never will. And I'll be the first one to acknowledge that different things work for different parents and different children. There is no one-size-fits-all, magic guide to being a good parent.

Don't forget—the lessons, values, and advice contained in the previous chapters very much apply to parenting. The goal is to live out these principles ourselves and ultimately pass them on to the next generation, as well.

I'm also a big believer in the old adage that it takes a village to raise a child. Everyone needs support along the way. My hope is that some of the advice Wesley and I have picked up during our parenting journey thus far can help you in yours one day, the same way we have received help from family and friends over the years.

A UNITED FRONT

Disagreements happen in marriage, and it's common to have different opinions than your spouse from time to time on how to approach certain aspects of parenting and situations in general. However, it's important to always stand with your spouse on parenting decisions. Don't disagree on these things in front of the kids. Otherwise, you'll undermine the decision (and any lesson they should be learning from it) and your children will start trying to pit one parent against the other whenever they want to get their own way.

Put up a united front to your kids, whether you agree in private or not.

TOUGH LOVE

Both Wesley and I learned a lot from each of our parents. They taught us timeless lessons and values when we were younger—things we can now implement ourselves as parents. They might not have realized it back then when raising us, but they were also preparing us to raise their future grandkids the entire time. Some of their lessons were the kinds of things we only saw the wisdom in after the distance of time allowed us to step back and gain fresh perspective—the perspective of parents. Perhaps chief among those important, yet hard to learn, lessons was the benefit of tough love.

My mom undoubtedly put this into practice—she earned her nickname of "Stone Cold" when my sisters and I were growing up. But everything she did was for our benefit. Both in life's everyday routines and its big moments, she taught us to think critically and be self-sufficient.

Make Them Put the Shoe on the Other Foot

I can vividly remember one particular experience that was illustrative of my mom's consistent approach.

In third grade, I had a teacher that would just never call on me when she asked a question in class. I was doing what I thought was my best to get called on—but she just wouldn't do it. I tried and tried some more. But as weeks passed with the same results, I grew increasingly confused and frustrated. One day, I'd had enough.

I complained to my mom, "Why won't she call on me?"

Mom turned it right back around on me. "Why do *you* think she's not calling on you?"

I tried to ignore the question and kept complaining. She wasn't being fair, I said.

"That's what you say," my mom responded. "But what would *she* say right now? What would she tell me that you're not telling me?"

She continued to tell me to put the shoe on the other foot. She challenged me to think about my teacher's perspective and how the situation might look from her vantage point. There is always another side to a story, she reminded me.

"Have you considered that she isn't calling on you because she wants to give other students a chance to answer? Maybe she knows that you already know the answers," Mom said. "You can't just think about yourself—because everything isn't about you."

My mom then effectively told me to control what I could control.

"Could you be doing something differently to get called on?" she quizzed me. "Are you being polite and respectful? If I could see what you're doing in class, would you be proud of it?"

Moments like those with my mom taught me to never feel sorry for myself and to always take responsibility for what I could have done or could be doing differently to help achieve my desired outcome. She constantly asked me, "What would the other person tell me?" And then she followed it up with, "Well, how much truth is there in that?"

It got to the point where I would think of her questions in the moment. And sometimes that would help me reposition my thought process as I acted—often allowing for a different or better outcome.

She wanted me to see the other side and what I could do to create a better situation or relationship. It fostered a mentality in me that I was never a victim. Rather, I was always in control of how I handled what was before me and therefore what was possible. Little did I know growing up how valuable that lesson was. Not only is it something that helped me develop personally, it's now something that I try to pass on to Bennett and Ridgeway.

Make Them Handle the Little Things

Another parenting lesson I learned firsthand from my mom is the importance of letting (and making) kids handle the little things by themselves. While we wish our children could stay young and be under our roofs forever, everything we do as parents is ultimately preparing them for the rest of their lives—including their lives away from home.

This is why we need to put our children in positions from an early age in which they can't rely on us (and other people in general) to do everything for them. Gradually, they need to learn to handle themselves and navigate situations independently. It might come off as tough to them in the moment, but they'll thank you later.

My mom did this in the most minor ways—we didn't even realize it was happening most of the time. In practice, this can be as small as making your child order their own food at a restaurant. Or having them explain directly to their basketball coach why they'll need to miss practice. As parents, we're not doing our jobs by doing those things for them. Our job is to prepare them to handle those things by themselves—equip them with what they need and then empower them to do it.

Involve Them in Decision-Making

One of the core life skills they're going to need is knowing how to make decisions. This starts from an early age. Again, start small. Give your children choices—even the tiniest decision points are building blocks. I have watched my sister, Janie, and, my brother-in-law, Chase, do this with their three children from the earliest age, and it makes a huge difference. *Do you want me to read you X book or Y book tonight? It is time to get in the car. Do you want the white shoes or the red ones?* They'll be given the confidence that this small power entails, but they'll also learn their decisions have consequences. This means when they make a decision, make them own it and stick with it.

Once you've built up from the small decisions, involve them in larger decisions. For example, Wesley and I try to be very intentional about involving Bennett and Ridgeway in the dialogue regarding decisions that affect our family unit. It helps for them to be able to practice weighing tangible pros and cons of real situations that directly impact them. Not every conversation or decision has to be as big as whether or not to run for the US Senate. But don't hesitate to use everyday, real-life choices as learning opportunities.

Be Big on the "Why"

A key part of effective decision-making is the ability to think critically. For children to learn how to make good decisions, they need to understand the reasoning involved in ultimately arriving at a decision.

It can take some patience in the moment, but it's well worth it in the long run to walk children through your reasoning whenever possible. The key word here is, "*Why?*" Challenge them to ask it themselves (politely and when appropriate, of course), and proactively explain to them the answer to that very question.

Take time to outline *why* we do things a certain way, *why* a certain rule exists, and *why* we are disappointed in something that they did. One of Wesley's parenting pillars is to try to never tell our kids, "Because we said so." While that answer should suffice from the perspective of instilling discipline and children being respectful, we also want them to understand the logic behind the "*what.*" Ultimately, if they come to understand the underlying reasoning, they can make better decisions in the future.

Make Them Wait

Patience is definitely a virtue—and it's not just important for parents. We need to instill it in our children, too.

In today's age of instant gratification, this can be especially challenging. But it is a necessary and valuable lesson to learn from a young age.

The age of Amazon and the ease of finding things online has changed so much. Whereas it would take me weeks to figure out where to get those cool new shoes my friend was wearing—and even then, I would likely have to wait for Christmas or my birthday to get them—children today can instantaneously find them in stores across the country the very day they see them and have them in their home and on their feet two days after a click. The ease to purchase certainly has its benefits, but instilling patience is not one of them. To teach this, make your children wait for things. Make them work for things, too. Again, start with the little ones and build up.

That new video game they want? *Not right now, but if you do well on your next three tests and your semester grade comes out where we discussed it should, ask me again.* That new outfit? *Save up your allowance, and then you can buy it for yourself.*

If the good things in life come easily and come quickly, we don't get nearly as much satisfaction out of them compared to when we have to wait for them—and when we have to earn them. So, make them wait.

Nothing Good Happens after Midnight

Life is full of temptations and difficult situations. First, we should strive to teach our kids to avoid them whenever they're foreseeable. Nothing good happens after midnight, for example, so go home. But it's not always that simple.

Navigating life at any age can be a challenge, but it's especially trying as our children grow up. We can equip them with decision-making skills and critical thinking ability all we want, but social pressures can override these lessons in the moment.

One thing that my mom taught me—and something that is still seared in my brain today—is to ask yourself, "Would I be comfortable with my grandparents seeing me act like this or saying that?" If the answer is no, it's probably something we shouldn't be doing at all. And just because others are doing it doesn't mean we have to or should join in.

It's important for children to have this kind of perspective to fall back on. Before they text, before they post, before they act, plant that question in their head, so they can always come back to it when they need it most.

And just like my dad has always told me, remind your children, "You will never do wrong by doing right."

Make Them Go to the Bathroom, Even if They Don't Have To

I'll keep this one short and sweet. We've all been there. We just left the house, the grocery store, the stadium, or wherever we were with the kids. Whether we have a long drive ahead of us or it's just a trip across town, seemingly without fail we soon hear from the back-seat, "Can we stop? I really need to go to the bathroom."

Make them use the bathroom before you get in the car. Don't ask, "Does anyone *need* to go to the bathroom before we leave?" Make it a directive. "Everyone try and use the bathroom before we head out, because we're not stopping once we're in the car." I promise that you won't regret it.

IT'S OK TO NOT BE OK

Parents, this is an important one. And it's something we all have to remind ourselves from time to time.

It's ok to not be ok.

We all want to be indestructible and unflinching in front of our children—and in front of the world. However, if you are struggling individually, the best thing you can do for your children and your family is to get help. This is a sign of true strength, not weakness. If you don't take care of yourself, you will not be able to take care of them. It may be as simple as asking friends or family to help give you a much-needed break, or you may need to sit down with a professional to help you work through everything. Either way, there is absolutely nothing to be ashamed of, so be honest with yourself and your family. Treatment works—and it's worth it.

You Are Not Alone

While parenting can seem like a thankless job at times, know that you are never alone. There are countless people out there, many who have previously dealt with similar situations to the ones you are facing now, who would be happy to help. But it's hard for people to assist you if you don't ask for it or welcome it.

Don't be afraid to ask for advice. Whether it's older relatives, your "walking group," or your neighbors, lean on others for counsel, perspective, and support.

I remember sitting in that Boston hospital room with Bennett, this newborn baby, in my arms thinking, "You're not actually going to send me home with her, are you?" I mean, I knew *nothing* about this parenting thing. But that's how it is for almost every parent the first time.

The best resources in parenting are often those who have recently experienced it themselves. Ask early and often, because chances are people you know found themselves in a similar spot, asking themselves the same kinds of questions—and they might just have found the answers you need.

USE IT OR LOSE IT

Time is an incredible gift from God. But we also have a responsibility to use it wisely.

This truth is no different when it comes to parenting. In fact, this reality is only magnified. We have limited time with our children, and we're called to be intentional about how we use every second of it.

Even some of the simplest moments can be significant. My most treasured—and impactful—childhood memories didn't happen at Disney World or on a fancy vacation, they actually occurred around a tiny kids' table sitting in our kitchen. My parents got my sisters and me a small, dark-brown rectangular table and four chairs that were *just* our size. Even though he didn't exactly fit, my dad would make it common practice to sit with us and eat. He would remind us to keep both feet on the floor, chew with our mouths closed, and keep one hand and our napkin on our lap.

In addition to instilling good table manners, he artfully taught us how to properly carry on conversation by asking us about our day, coloring assignment, or playtime. We loved our time with Dad during those meals. I can still picture him sitting across from me and asking me to pass the butter. Even in the most ordinary moments in our kitchen, he was laying a firm foundation on which we could stand tall.

Enjoy Every Stage of Life

Life gets busy, and time flies. It can be easy to let seconds turn to minutes, and soon years have zipped by without us realizing it.

We have a natural tendency in a given moment to be focused on trying to just get through that moment. We fixate on and worry about the challenges directly in front of us. Ironically, what we might not realize in that moment is those very challenges will be what we miss once they're behind us. Then we blink, and that's exactly what's happened as life transitions into a new season.

Every stage of our children's lives brings new and unique challenges. Newborn, toddler, "big kid," pre-teen, teenager—they're all different, and they're all challenging. This is a hard thing, but some of the challenges of today become the things you miss tomorrow. Find ways to deal with the issues at hand while still enjoying the moment.

Your child might be a similar age to Bennett and Ridgeway—the stage in which travel sports is a big feature. That can be challenging logistically, financially, and because of the time commitment. However, we should enjoy every waking minute of it. One day (sooner than we'd like), we'll be empty nesters pining for these days of travel ball—and the quality time spent with our fellow travel sports families.

I have already experienced this dynamic with earlier stages of my children's respective childhoods. I know as a new momma, first with Bennett as a newborn and then with Ridgeway when I had two babies to raise, I was guilty of being in a constant fog. I was so laser-focused on surviving each day that I neglected to take in the moments each day offered. Now, there are days when I wish Bennett and Ridgeway were that age again. I wish I could go back and hold them as babies—to sing their favorite lullabies, read their favorite nursery rhymes, and play their favorite games.

Whichever stage you're in, don't let the moment pass you by before you enjoy it. Love the joys and the challenges alike.

Try to Say "Yes"

We get so busy in life that it's easy to say, "Not right now." But I promise you the moment they stop asking is the moment you will wish you had said, "Yes." Not only do we want to not miss out on making memories with our children, but there is also power in just saying that one three-letter word.

I have been working on this recently. As I write this, just the other day Bennett asked me to go on a run with her. Now, I only run if someone is chasing me. However, I thought to myself, *She may never ask me to do this with her again.* So, I said that word. *Yes.* We stayed side-by-side in our first few strides, and then it wasn't long before she began to outpace me. I am pretty sure her favorite part was figuring the length of time between her arrival back at the house and mine.

I thought the same thing with Ridgeway when he asked me to play him one on one in basketball. *When is he going to ask his mom to play anything with him again?* I tried to get him interested in an old-fashioned game of HORSE, but he wasn't having it. So, I said that word. *Yes.* I knew that would mean a guarantee that I couldn't walk for the next three days. But when is he going to ask me to do that again?

The question could come in any number of forms. They might ask you to do a puzzle with them or play a game. But the answer we should try our best to reach is a constant. *Yes.*

Life has so many demands. It might not seem like a pressing request in the moment; however, I'd encourage you to not lose sight of the realities of time. If your child is asking you to be a part of their activity, their day, and their memory, you will never regret doing so. Build memories and spend time with them, even if it is not what you envisioned.

That email can be answered 15 minutes down the line. That phone call can wait a little bit. That person's social media post will still be there (and if it's not, your friend will have the screenshot to show you). There is time later to go grocery shopping. But that high-five after Ridgeway beat me in our basketball game can never be replaced.

Strength in Numbers

If you have more than one child, raise them to be teammates. Stress the importance of having each other's backs and them always being able to turn to each other throughout life's seasons. Your kids should level with each other, encourage each other, and help each other make good decisions. Wesley even tells Bennett and Ridgeway that you'll get in less trouble if you make a mistake together than if you make one on your own.

I learned early on that friends can come and go, but that my siblings—Jackson, Janie, and Norma—would always be my ride-or-die. Four girls that span eight years lead many to comment, "I bet it was challenging growing up in your house with all those girls," or "No doubt, y'all must fight all the time." I think each one of us takes great pride in being able to tell people that those assumptions are absolutely incorrect.

Growing up, we created a special bond. We saw each other as a unit and both took pride in each other's successes and responsibility for each other's failures. Instead of exploiting each other's weaknesses, we each found ways to use our own unique strengths to build one another up. There is no dominant sibling, which means we all take turns leading—a different sister will step out in front depending on the challenge or situation at hand.

Without hesitation, I tell you that one of the greatest gifts God has given me is the ability to do life with these three remarkable women. If you have more than one child, make it your goal for them to say that about their siblings, too.

To Each Their Own

Remember that your children are individuals. Don't expect one to be a carbon copy of another.

When you have multiple children, creating unique, individualized spaces to engage with each child is incredibly important. My friend Jamie has seven kids, and among the many things she excels at is carving out individual time to bond with each of her children. This is a crucial thing for every parent to be intentional about.

Even if it's just a one-on-one trip to the store, that time together is meaningful and needed for their development and confidence. It also helps you as a parent learn more about each child as an individual. Your time can be spent solely on them, rather than refereeing between your children or managing group dynamics. Additionally, it'll create distinctive memories neither of you will soon forget.

Pray in the Moment

Speaking of Jamie, another parenting lesson that I have picked up from her is teaching our children to pray in the moment.

When you see something happen—pray about it. It could be something that elicits sadness or fear. It could be something about which you are happy. Either way, we should be teaching our children to keep their eyes on the Lord at all times.

It's also important to pray *for* people in the moment—and let them know. I am blessed with people in my life who tell me that they're praying for me. Sometimes they mention it in person or on a phone call, and other times it's a quick text of encouragement. No matter the medium of how they let me know, it's a wonderfully uplifting thing for me—and an empowering one for the person on the giving end.

Similarly, there is unspeakable power in praying *with* people in the moment. If you see someone struggling with a heartbreak or adversity, ask them if you can take a moment to pray with them. Words can't describe how much it meant to me on the campaign trail to have complete strangers ask if they could pause to pray with me.

That's the kind of behavior our children can see. They're studying us all of the time, whether we realize it or not. My sister, Norma, and my brother-in-law, Daniel, are so diligent about this with their little ones, and it is inspiring to watch.

Imagine if we raised a new generation of prayer warriors in America. The values and examples we set for our children matter.

Phones Down, Eyes and Ears Up

In this age of smartphones and social media, we can lose our grasp of what a moment actually is.

I'll admit that I've been guilty of this myself. A few months ago, Bennett had to set me straight after I got a little too wrapped up in taking pictures of a family outing instead of being fully present in the outing itself. "Can we just have a moment without you trying to capture it?" she asked. She was right.

We can't forget as parents to remind ourselves to prioritize experiencing the moment. I'm all for finding ways to preserve the moment, but be mindful of who are you trying to preserve it for and if that is ultimately worth it.

Focus on Your Own Timeline

This is another area where we all can improve. From time to time, we fall into the trap of not being present in the moment because we're engrossed with our phone and watching what's happening in someone else's life through social media.

Our time with our children is fleeting. Do we really want to use too much of it scrolling through other people's pictures and posts?

Instead, let's make memories of our own with our children and build our own timeline.

The same advice we often give our kids applies to us as parents, too. Put those phones down at the dinner table. Don't just sit among your family; be with them in that moment.

Educate Yourself—and Them

A lot has changed since my generation was growing up. The advent of social media, the smartphone, and the front-facing camera, along with the evolution (*devolution*, really) of the internet have made cyberspace a more and more dangerous place for our children.

It's key for us as parents to be proactively engaged in this space, especially because it is one thing we did not have to grapple with when we were their age (at least to the same degree). To be able to do this effectively, we first need to educate ourselves. We have to know the score about the latest in social media platforms and technology that will affect our children's lives (AI is next, folks). Then, we can have meaningful conversations with them about the pros and cons involved, and we can set healthy boundaries and guard rails to help keep them safe and making good decisions.

The dangers and challenges of social media usage and how kids now communicate digitally is something that pops up consistently among fellow moms I know. We talk about the latest incidents occurring with our families, in their schools, or in our community. The horror stories are heartbreaking. There are cases of what I call "virtual eggings"—such as people creating anonymous burner accounts simply to cyberbully peers. And there are children and teenagers who make youthful mistakes that they can't hide from—like sending around a picture of themselves they can never take back.

Now, the data is finally beginning to catch up to the harsh reality families have been dealing with in recent years.

Just this year, the US Surgeon General released an extensive advisory on social media usage that warns in part, "Extreme, inappropriate, and harmful content continues to be easily and widely accessible by children and adolescents. This can be spread through direct pushes, unwanted content exchanges, and algorithmic designs."

The report points to research linking increased social media usage among children with significantly heightened risks of poor mental health outcomes. Across the board, the statistics don't lie. The CDC's Youth Risk Behavior Survey found that 57% of high school girls and 29% of high school boys felt persistently sad or hopeless in 2021. The CDC also found that 1 in 3 high school girls seriously considered attempting suicide last year, while 9% of high school students actually attempted death by suicide in the same time period.

There is no doubt that this is a full-blown crisis. Along with Senators Tom Cotton, Brian Schatz, and Chris Murphy (all fellow parents of school-aged children), I have introduced the Protecting Kids on Social Media Act. We're working hard to pass this important piece of bipartisan legislation, but we also know that solutions are only going to be successful if parents step up and take charge in their own households when it comes to social media.

As parents, sometimes we have to do hard things. This is one of them.

Memories Can Last Forever

While we don't want to prioritize preserving a memory over creating a memory, one of the benefits of technology is the enhanced, easy-to-use tools at our fingertips that can help us preserve moments in time for eternity.

One thing I like to do is right after something happens in my family life—no, not while it's happening—is to make a record of it on my phone. We all like to think we will remember the moments—the things our children said, what they did, and how it all happened. But the truth is we won't be able to recall everything years from now (or even months from now).

Don't be afraid to use the notes app on your phone to jot those things down when you get a free moment and they're still fresh in your head. Or, record a voice memo of you or a loved one talking about what just happened.

Finally, and *yes* this is me being a hopelessly sentimental mom, capture those pictures and videos on your phone—then consider making time to print them out or create a simple photo album each year—just don't let that process take away from the moment itself.

Years and decades from now, you'll be glad you did.

CHAPTER 15

Stand Back Up

It was January 18, 2023. The previous day marked two weeks since I was sworn into office as Alabama's US Senator.

That winter Wednesday around lunchtime, I walked into Dunbar Magnet School in downtown Mobile. I was coming from a productive meeting with local, state, and federal law enforcement officials from across Coastal Alabama.

This was my first ever state work period (a designated timeframe when the Senate is not in session in Washington), and I'd chosen Dunbar as one of my maiden visits as Senator. This public middle school serves more than 500 students across grades six through eight, with an academic focus on creative and performing arts.

When I walked through the front door and got to the main hallway, I immediately felt at home. Those squeaky floors and locker-lined walls brought back the memories from my days at Coppinville Junior High in Enterprise.

From the minute I arrived, I was inspired and uplifted by the people around me—students and educators alike. I was greeted warmly by administrators and teachers in the hallway, along with a few impressive students participating in the school's journalism course. They introduced themselves with confidence and professionalism, before proceeding to interview me on camera. These student journalists could have handled a gig in the hallways of the Capitol without a problem—*actually*, they probably could teach many of the "pros" a thing or two.

My time at the school was off to an energizing start, and the inspiration didn't stop there. As I walked down the hallway, I spotted a large posterboard display featuring various student projects on American electoral history—and, *oh wow*, that's *my picture* right there on that wall. Talk about surreal.

I visited a dance class. I walked in as they were in the middle of rehearsing for an upcoming performance. The memories of Mom's dance studio came flooding back.

Then it was time to visit a civics class, where I got what were tougher questions than almost anything I faced on the campaign trail. These students weren't lobbing softballs. They were sharp, respectful, conscientious, and well-prepared—*that's* a good change-up!

Finally, it was time to head into the gym for a schoolwide assembly. I entered from the end furthest from the stage, where the band and chorus were positioned behind a lectern. I walked forward, among the sea of uniforms filling the bleachers on either side, and took my seat at the front. It dawned on me right then that all these students were there to hear *from me*—I wasn't simply a part of a regularly scheduled gathering.

That's when they began to play "The Climb." The goosebumps were immediate. They couldn't have known what a fitting song choice they had made.

"*I can almost see it*," the students sang. "*That dream I'm dreaming. But there's a voice inside my head saying, 'You'll never reach it.'*"

That's pretty much when I could feel the tears welling up. The reality of where I was—and where I had come from—really hit me.

Then, their message really hit home a few verses later. "*The struggles I'm facing, the chances I'm taking, sometimes might knock me down. But no, I'm not breaking.*"

The emotion of the moment wasn't something I could hide—and I didn't try.

This is why I ran. *They* are why I ran.

Once their beautiful rendition of the song had finished, my niece, Kaitlyn, got up and began introducing me. She was a teacher at the school and had originally put Dunbar on my radar over the Christmas holiday. Hearing her talk to our family about the school's mission, I could immediately tell how proud she was of her students and colleagues. She couldn't stop bragging about those kids—and I was eager to see why. Of course, my visit—*unsurprisingly*—showed me how right she was to be so proud.

It was my time to take up the microphone.

I told them why I ran for the Senate—because of young people like them. I want my kids, and all children across our great nation, to be able to live their American Dreams. I want the unseen to be seen. And, ultimately, I got off the sidelines to fight for Alabama's and America's future.

I shared what I believe. For example, that each and every child across our nation—regardless of their zip code—deserves access to a high-quality education. That's the key to unlocking the American

Dream. I discussed how impressed I was by them—and how proud I was of them. In the time I had already spent with them, it was clear how talented they were—and that their innovative school and hardworking educators were doing tremendous work to help them reach their full potential.

And we talked about many of the same lessons, values, and tips of advice I've shared with you in these chapters. This is always my favorite part of speaking to groups of students like this, whether it was the young people at Dunbar that day or those at the likes of University Charter School in Livingston, i3 Academy in Birmingham, Alabama Christian Academy in Montgomery, or the Boys and Girls Clubs of America's *Summit for America's Youth* in Washington, DC.

I've spoken at different places, on different occasions, with different people who each have different experiences, backgrounds, circumstances, and stories. I'm sure that my life has been different than yours, just like it is distinctive from the unique lives of the thousands of students I've had the opportunity to visit with. But the universal principles we all need to practice are the same.

At Dunbar that afternoon, I told them to be confident.

Don't let your insecurities limit your potential. You're more prepared than you think. It's true that the world places limitations on each of us, but it is truly the ones we place on ourselves that do the most damage. Don't give away your power or confidence with your words or actions.

You are beneath no one. You are fearless. You belong.

I told them to be empowered and empowering.

Soak up others' info and gain knowledge. Participate and ask questions. You'll only get out of life what you put in. Support one another. Look for opportunities to encourage and empower others with the tools needed for success.

Remember—relationships matter, and there is absolutely no substitute for trust and respect.

Next, I encouraged them to be change agents instead of title holders.

Be open, be adventurous, and be bold. Challenge yourself to think about "why." Ask questions of your family members, pastor, teachers, and coaches.

Alabama has had our share of courageous change agents like John Lewis, Rosa Parks, and Helen Keller who have stood back up, done hard things, blazed new trails, and helped fulfill America's promise of forming a more perfect union. We're the home to innovators, engineers, and scientists who dared to dream of going where no person had ever gone. Told something was impossible, Alabamians have time and again defied the odds and expanded the bounds of human achievement. This is the state that launched NASA's Apollo program off the face of our planet and into the pages of history. Alabama is a place where not even the sky is the limit—where we shoot for the stars and land on the Moon (and one day soon, Mars, through NASA's next-generation Artemis program).

Back at Dunbar, I explained that's why we must be unafraid to fail.

While failure is not fun, it is an opportunity to grow professionally, personally, and intellectually. Failure is part of learning and ultimately succeeding.

In this great state and in this great country, you can achieve anything you set your mind to. With hard work, resiliency, faith, and the support of so many wonderful people, a public-school girl from the Wiregrass—this daughter of two small business owners—can grow up to be a United States Senator. That's the American Dream at work! It comes down to the opportunity to try and fail—and the opportunity to thrive. It's the hope of knowing that hard work can pay off in unimaginable ways.

I also urged those bright young students to be themselves—and be *their* best. The greatest joy you will ever have is the freedom to be yourself. Life comes down to a series of choices, and *you*—and *only you*—are in control of making them.

Remember, it's your character, your integrity, your work ethic, and the way you treat people.

You're in charge of writing the book you want written. And you will never reach your potential trying to be anyone but yourself.

I was nearing my conclusion now.

Close your eyes: Where do you want to be in 20 years?

Fighter pilot...teacher...public servant...rocket scientist...general...mom...doctor...police officer. The opportunities are endless.

Open your eyes. Now is your time. The question is not if you will change the world, but rather how you will change the world.

I want you to promise me a few things: One: leave this school year having challenged yourself. Two: leave here having overcome an obstacle. Three: leave here having helped someone else. Four: leave here having taken down a wall. Five: leave here having thought outside your box. Six: leave here having been inspired to make a difference. Seven: leave here having sought an understanding unlike your own. Eight: leave here seeing each other not as competition, but as iron sharpening iron. You should leave here knowing that just like yours, others' successes should be celebrated. Because we are all better for them.

And finally—this is the big one. Y'all are not just the leaders of the future, you are the now. And I'm here to tell you that we need you. Our state and our country need you.

I don't know what your life is going to look like. The obstacles and challenges you will face—and those you already have to face—will be your own. They'll be different than mine and different from the person sitting next to you.

But one thing I can promise that will be true for all of us: life will knock you down. It's knocked me down plenty of times. And the only reason—the only one—that I have the honor of being able to speak with you today is because I keep getting back up.

Will you stand back up?

I want you to make me a promise. You will stand back up. We'll say it together.

I. Will. Stand. Back. Up.

Those students at Dunbar repeated the refrain, with the participation growing even louder. It brought the house down. Kids were literally standing back up. They were on their feet, jumping up and down—smiles from ear to ear.

"I will stand back up!" To hear those children enthusiastically continue to say those five crucial words left an imprint on my heart and reaffirmed an undeniable purpose for me to pursue.

I stepped down from the stage and waded into the waves of students coming to me.

I think that's the best received I've ever been after a speech. For what felt like the next 45 minutes, I was posing for selfies, giving out bearhugs, high-fiving, fist-bumping, practicing shaking hands and using eye contact, and hearing students—these amazing kids I had never met before—tell me that they love me and that they would *stand back up*. I had more events to get to before the day was out, but I wish I could've stayed there for hours.

That night as I was headed home, I couldn't stop thinking about

Dunbar—about those young people and their reaction to being told to stand back up. It's what we all need to get through life's valleys—and it's what we as a nation must do to confront the ever-changing challenges of this century.

Every generation is called to do hard things. While we don't yet know what this next generation's charge will entail, we can be assured that God will call. Each iteration is different—but the guide to answering that call remains the same.

It's about digging down deep and having the will, the courage, and the fight to stand back up.

Some of the things before us may seem overwhelming or even impossible. But remember that we can overcome anything through Him.

"*Perhaps you were born for such a time as this*," Esther 4:14 proclaims.

This is our time for choosing.

Think about the Greatest Generation and those who stormed the beaches of Normandy on D-Day. I had the opportunity to visit Omaha Beach and Pointe du Hoc a few years ago. Reading about it is one thing, but seeing the steepness of those cliffs really put in perspective the magnitude of what those brave souls faced.

In 1944, the Greatest Generation didn't stare up at those cliffs and turn back. They pushed forward and climbed, because they knew our country, our values, and our liberties were worth it.

This is a tale as old as time. History has been written by the resiliency and fortitude of men and women who got knocked down in different ways. But we know their stories because they did not stay down. We are *here* because they stood back up.

Stand Back Up

We will get knocked down in our lifetime. I guarantee it. But we have a choice in what we do next.

What I can promise you is this: we *will* stand back up. America always does, because Americans always do. We have an obligation larger than ourselves. The stakes are high, yet the potential rewards are even greater. We have it in our power to create the world in which we want future generations to live. Let's make sure that America's best days are yet to come.

It's our time to answer the call. It's our turn to do *hard things*.

ACKNOWLEDGMENTS

As mentioned in the previous pages, no one gets anywhere alone. And my life is no exception. My opportunity to serve as a US Senator is the direct result of *a lot* of people doing *a lot* of things. To everyone who has poured love into me throughout my lifetime, I am beyond grateful for your time, energy, support, and direction. To those who believed that this was possible and worked diligently to make it happen—in every corner of the state—I am so thankful for your unwavering effort and willingness to put it all on the line.

To my husband, who *literally* put it all on the line to walk through this journey with me every single day, who is the rock of our family and believed in what was possible, who is my partner in all things, and who, as evidenced throughout the pages of this book, has an immediate impact on everyone he meets...

To our children, who not only encouraged me to step into the arena and do a hard thing, but who have conducted themselves with such grace and grit as we have navigated a challenging campaign and *now* the Senate schedule. You give up things every day so that our family can serve. Your dad and I believe you both to be incredibly special, and we could not be prouder of who each of you are...

To my parents, who taught me important life lessons and encouraged me through good times and challenging ones, who instilled in me that the most important things in life are faith, family, and freedom. You helped to build the foundation that I am standing on today. Without your sacrifice, your example, and your love, none of this is possible...

To my sisters, who God blessed me to be able to do life with and who stood in there with me through it all. I am inspired by each of you and grateful for our incredible bond. Y'all are my people...

To my grandparents, both here on earth and the ones watching from above who were willing to plant trees whose shade they knew they would never sit in. So much of who I am is because of you...

To my aunts and uncles, who helped to guide me and who have supported me throughout life's journey...

To my cousins, who most of my childhood memories involve—whether at the Pond House or at Lake Seminole. God gave us a great crew, and I cherish walking alongside y'all...

To Wesley's parents, who welcomed me with open arms into the family, who sacrificed for Wesley to achieve, and who have continued to point him to the Lord throughout life...

To my brothers-in-law and my sisters-in-law who support and love *not just* Wesley and me, but so importantly, our children...

To my nieces and nephews, I hope there are some nuggets in this book that are helpful to you as you, just like my own children, navigate life's ups and downs...

To my friends, from childhood to college to adulthood, and everything in between...

To my teachers, mentors, previous coworkers, and Girls State family...

To the volunteers on our US Senate campaign, who spread the word and truly helped us build out authentic grassroots...

To our campaign team, Katie Walsh Shields, Paul Shashy,

Elizabeth Williams, Sean Ross, Clint Reid, Collyn Davis, Rachel Leppert, Andrea Hutchings, John Annesley DeGaris, John Henry Woods, and Bailee Sneed. Y'all are the very best. Several of you took these jobs despite some people saying it would be career ending—and each of you put heart and soul into our campaign each day to ensure we would have the very best chance of success...

To Clay Armentrout, who agreed to serve as Chief of Staff and has done an outstanding job opening the doors of our office. Clay works diligently to ensure our vision is executed *daily* so that we put Alabama and the nation in a better place as a result of our service...

To the man—Senator Richard Shelby, and his wonderful wife Dr. Annette Shelby—whose seat I have filled but whose shoes will likely never fit. He gave me a shot almost 20 years ago. Senator Shelby will always be Alabama's greatest statesman, leaving a lasting legacy of fighting for this nation and an imprint on our great state that will ALWAYS remain...

This book has been a journey in and of itself. And just like my life, this book had its own walking group.

To Matt Latimer, who first approached me about writing something down on paper.

To Sean Desmond, who took the time to get to know me and saw the vision of what this project could be—who guided me and the team through this journey with grace and a steady hand.

To Joe Hack, who kept everyone and *everything* on track. Joe not only understood the vision but helped to ensure this project stayed true to it. And he believed in what was possible, long before most.

To Sean Ross, who is talented beyond measure with instincts to match. Sean took a leap of faith of his own to work on our campaign, and I am fortunate to continue to benefit from his wise counsel daily. He knew my story and helped me determine the best way to tell it.

To Fleet Cooper, who did an outstanding job directing the audio book (he also knows I am holding out hope for a Sweet Home Alabama II!).

To Troy University; Chancellor Jack Hawkins; President Pro Tempore of the Board of Trustees, Gibson Vance; Senior Vice Chancellor Brig. Gen. Rick Boutwell, USAF ret.; Montgomery campus Vice Chancellor Ray White; Matthew Clower; Kyle Gassiott; Michelle Mowery; and Austin Toy, each of whom made the audiobook possible. These Alabamians worked with an unpredictable schedule and allowed me to use their incredible facilities at Troy University's Montgomery campus so that I could record this audiobook at home, in the great state of Alabama.

To each of you, I say THANK YOU. Without y'all, this project would not have been possible. Thank you for lending your incredible talents to make this all happen. I am truly grateful for the time, energy, and passion you dedicated into putting this story on shelves and into air pods around the United States.

It is my hope that others will be encouraged and inspired through the words on these pages—that someone will think more is possible and will have the courage to stand back up. I am blessed to share my story and lessons I have learned from a lifetime's worth of people who have my *immeasurable* gratitude.

From the bottom of my heart, with every ounce of me, THANK YOU.

ABOUT THE AUTHOR

Katie Boyd Britt is an American politician, attorney, and businesswoman who was elected to the United States Senate from Alabama in 2022. She previously served as president and CEO of the Business Council of Alabama from 2018 to 2021, as well as chief of staff for US Senator Richard Shelby from 2016 to 2018.